ALLERTON PARK INSTITUTE

Number 31

Papers Presented at the Allerton Park Institute

Sponsored by

University of Illinois
Graduate School of Library and Information Science

held

October 29-31, 1989
Allerton Conference Center
Robert Allerton Park
Monticello, Illinois

Ethics and the Librarian

F. W. LANCASTER

Editor

University of Illinois
Graduate School of Library and Information Science
Urbana-Champaign, Illinois

CONTENTS

Introduction

The Federal Bureau of Investigation was the catalyst that established the theme for the Twenty-First Allerton Institute, held at the University of Illinois at Urbana-Champaign's Allerton House, October 29-31, 1989. The FBI's Library Awareness Program, if it had any merit, did raise a significant ethical conflict between the librarian's responsibility to preserve the confidentiality surrounding use of library materials and his or her responsibility as a citizen of the United States. The FBI's activities, along with an apparent increase in interest in ethical matters in society as a whole, suggested "professional ethics" as an appropriate theme for a conference of librarians in 1989.

Of course, confidentiality of records is not the only ethical issue facing the library profession. In organizing this conference, members of the planning committee endeavored to identify speakers who could cover a wide range of ethical issues—in relationships with the public, with vendors, with city officials, in the management of human resources within the library, in the reference function of libraries, in how the library's resources should be allocated in order to satisfy minority as well as majority interests, in how ethical issues should be presented to students of library science, and so on. The committee also attempted to bring in some ethical questions more peripheral to the library profession, as exemplified by the keynote address by Clifford Christians and the paper by Robert Hauptman. Since the sessions were received with enthusiasm by the participants, the planning committee feels that the conference itself was very successful, and hopes that the published proceedings may be of interest and value to a wider community of librarians.

The author is grateful to the other members of the planning committee, Professors Terry Weech and Robert Burger, for their help in designing the program and otherwise contributing to the success of the Institute.

F. W. LANCASTER
Editor

CLIFFORD G. CHRISTIANS

Director, Institute of Communications Research
University of Illinois at Urbana-Champaign

Information Ethics in a Complicated Age

INTRODUCTION

The old order of kinship and social class in Europe broke apart during the nineteenth century. Two revolutions gave the final blow: mass democracy and industrialism. Together, these explosive forces reversed the direction of Western society on the Continent and in North America.

The political revolution in France and the Industrial Revolution in Great Britain and the United States shifted the course of history around the North Atlantic. Presently, another revolution equal in power is reshaping the social contours. Past revolutions highlight the transformation taking place now: a cultural metamorphosis comparable in importance to mass democracy and technological industry one century earlier. The years may not appear as volatile, but the present modifications in our social structure are as extensive and substantial as those of the 1800s.

A DUALITY

How shall this contemporary phenomenon be labelled? Post-industrialism? A communications revolution? The information age? Telematics? A paperless society?

Such designations are insufficient. Unique to the modern day is global technology on a worldwide scale, and the two most decisive are in fundamental contradiction. Information technology has created global communication networks that potentially involve us all in each other's business. But its opposite, military technology, threatens the human race with annihilation. Today's global age has the technological sophistication dialectically to destroy all humanity while simultaneously binding all

3

nations into a worldwide information network. Since imminent destruction is now a possibility, scholarship in information ethics needs an urgency about it unlike any previous theorizing. Principial claims must henceforth embrace the needs of the entire human race within their purview.

1945: Nuclear technology, in principle, is now able to totalize the planet. 1957: Sputnik rockets into space, but not merely as a satellite fired from the U.S.S.R. in secret; the whole world is watching. The late Marshall McLuhan (1974) noted that Sputnik bound together humankind for the first time electronically. Lincoln's assassination took months to reach the London streets; a century later, Russian technology was paraded instantly before an admiring world. November 1963: The world participates as one in President Kennedy's funeral. Television, radio, and satellites gather us around the casket with all the emotion and ceremony of every burial. The parade down Pennsylvania Avenue occurs on Main Street, the World.

Since those heady days, Earth's orbits are loaded with satellites of information and for military deployment. In era number three, global technology stands in counterpoint: As information is increased, facilitation of global understanding is presumed. When the nuclear arms race is successfully curbed, these two technologies are put on the proper trajectory. Open information unfettered globally and destructive technology restrained politically yields a working formula for sustaining the globe at this auspicious moment of human history, although the relationship between improved information and decreased danger is porous at best.

That, in sanitized form, is the San Andreas fault line on which our technological civilization rests. But the problem is slightly more complicated.

Jacques Ellul (1981) developed the argument that the technological phenomenon is decisive, though not exclusive, in defining twentieth-century culture. As an explanatory element, it plays the part of capital in Marx's interpretation of the nineteenth century. This does not mean that technology has the same function as capital nor that the capitalist system is a thing of the past. It still exists, but capital no longer fulfills the role Marx claimed for it. Whereas work produces value for him, in industrially condensed societies the determining factor is technology. This creates value now and is not peculiar to capitalism. The characters have changed. Society can no longer be divided into capitalists and workers; the phenomenon is completely different and more abstract. Technological systems are now on one side and all humanity is on the other, the former driven by necessity and the human demand for freedom. Ellul concludes that the world in which we live must be read, not in terms of political-economic structures, but in terms of technology (ch. 2). While this analysis privileges the industrial order, even that three-fourths of the world which is not yet technological finds itself defined within technological parameters.

Thus the bipolar model needs to be restated. Global technologies of communications and extinction have given the present age its peculiar resonance; but the fundamental issue is the technological artifice within these boundaries which now defines the human habitat. The revolution today is that the world has entered a technological civilization. Technology is not merely one more arena for philosophers and sociologists to investigate, but a new foundation for understanding the self, human institutions, and ultimate reality. A society is technological, Ellul argues, not because of its machines, but from the pursuit of "machineness" in every area of human endeavor. Mechanistic techniques are applied not just to nature, but to social organizations and one's understanding of personhood. A technological society with global parameters separates itself from previous ones, including industrial civilizations, "through its historical consciousness that society is not fixed and given with the order of nature, but is an artificial human creation" (Fasching, n.d.). In this sense, finding an orientation in a technological civilization is fundamentally a religious problem. Unable to establish a meaningful existence outside the artificial ambience of a technological culture, human beings place their ultimate hope in it. Seeing no other source of security and failing to recognize the illusoriness of their technological freedom, they become slaves to the exacting determinations of efficiency.

Whereas previous social orders operated with a triad—humans/tools/nature—in technological societies, nature recedes and humans perceive themselves as living in a technical artifice, existing not in nature but in culture.

> Man does not any longer live in a natural environment but rather in a milieu composed of the products of his technology. . . . He can no longer take any significant action without technological inter-mediation. Technology constitutes an engulfing universe for man, who finds himself in it as in a cocoon. (Ellul, 1978, p. 216)

Our symbolic formations, or cultures, are now dominated by technological structures. In Ellul's framework, communications media represent the meaning-edge of the technological system, the arena where the latter's soul is most clearly exposed. Though exhibiting the structural elements of all technical artifacts, their particular identity as a technology inheres in their function as bearers of symbols. Information technologies thus incarnate the properties of technology while serving as agents for interpreting the meaning of the very phenomenon they embody. Ellul (1969) calls our communication systems the "innermost, and most elusive

manifestation" of human technological activity (p. xvii). All artifacts
communicate meaning in an important sense, but media instruments
carry this role exclusively. As the media sketch out our world, organize
our conversations, determine our decisions, and influence our self-
identity, they do so with a technological cadence, massaging in our souls
a technological rhythm and predisposition.

Over the centuries, in Western scholarship at least, ethicists could
take divine command theories seriously or, at a minimum, presume
various versions of Platonic absolutes. Even as these presumptions
unraveled in the nineteenth century, the immutability of nature, which
took care of itself and demonstrated physical permanence, made norms
of semi-enduring status at least imaginable. In other words, all previous
ethics reckoned only with noncumulative phenomena, directly or indi-
rectly. Morality could conceivably be the property of all, living as
humanity did on *terra firma* before the face of an Eternal Being, or at
least with a first principle that ordered the vacillations of everyday
affairs. But as Jacques Ellul, Ivan Illich and others have demonstrated,
a technological age is cumulative, expanding, and augmentative. Therefore, while endeavoring to form a new order of world understanding
through communications, one can simultaneously augment an artifice
where traditional ethical principles carry no resonance.

In his celebrated book, *The Imperative of Responsibility*, Hans Jonas
(1984) contends that today's ominous trends demand an entirely new
ethics: "Modern technology has introduced actions of such novel scale,
objects and consequences that the framework of former ethics can no
longer contain them" (p. 6). Jonas calls for a brawny, long-range ethics
commensurate with the extent of contemporary technological power.
But this presentation is not intended merely as a reprieve from minuscule
ethics. It takes Jonas' ideas full strength and resonates in somber tones
about the formidability of his challenge.

Conferences such as this are a priceless resource in a complicated
age. It is a hopeful sign that the same academic unit sponsoring the
Artificial Intelligence and Expert Systems (Lancaster & Smith, in press)
conference also organized this seminar on ethics. Professionals in information storage and transmission face a firestorm of issues at present,
and there are many impacted levels on which a sophisticated library
system operates today. Developing a library profession with integrity is
akin to building a home in a hurricane: the roof can never be safely
put in place given the whirlwind of demands and unending technological
innovations. And while a nine-session, two-day conference can help to
hammer out policy guidelines, get the ethical problems straight, and
stimulate each other's moral imagination, the larger context within
which we work is determined by the contours of the technological

civilization sketched above. It is essential that professional ethics—whether of librarians, journalists, engineers, doctors, or lawyers—be integrated into the common morality. Information ethics will prosper to the degree professional ethics as a whole develops a substantive and generative framework. Information professionals work in a fortuitous area that represents the quintessence of several axial issues at present, and are in a golden position to contribute to the debates in social ethics generally.

With praise to those who are lighting the proverbial candle rather than cursing the darkness, the author will describe the heavy clouds nonetheless—trusting that those in ethics for the long haul will use the seminal work this week to help unravel a conundrum and a paradox which makes our task in applied ethics nearly intractable.

A CONUNDRUM

In their commonplaces, industrialized countries presume that technology is merely a tool open to proper or improper use. As Oxford's R. A. Buchanan (1965) has written, "Technology is essentially amoral, a thing apart from values, an instrument which can be used for good or ill" (p. 163). A knife in a surgeon's hand saves a life and destroys it when used by a murderer. The same projector shows pornography and *National Geographic* specials. One is reminded of the familiar slogan, "Guns don't kill people, people do." In Swedish Lapland, snowmobiles are used for reindeer herding, among Canada's Eskimos for trapping, and in Wisconsin for leisure. Technological products are supposedly neutral and independent; they can support completely different cultures and lifestyles.

The presumption of neutrality has been very costly. It leads to an exaggerated, unbalanced emphasis on magnitude, control, uniformity, and integration—what Arnold Pacey calls the "virtuosity values" (p. 102). As a result, electronic communications are unreflectively trumped as the technological sublime and invested with divine significance. In its heaviest form, neutrality promotes a version of technological determinism in which technology's own inner logic appears to drive its development. This narrow view fosters the working rule that "If it can be done, it should be," eradicating other significant dimensions from decision-making.

The prevailing opinion that technology is neutral typically focuses on hardware—on tools and mechanical artifacts. That definition is starkly deficient in scope compared to technology as a value-laden human process. Technology is the distinct cultural activity in which human beings form and transform natural reality for practical ends. Given this perspective, valuing penetrates all technological activity, from the analytical framework used to understand technological issues, through the processes of design and fabrication, to the resulting tools and products. Although valuing surely involves the uses to which people put these technological objects, valuing saturates every phase prior to usage as well (Christians, 1989; Mosma, 1984).

There can be no isolated, neutral understanding of technology as though it exists in a presuppositionless vacuum. Instead, technology proceeds out of the whole of human experience and is directed by ultimate human commitments. Technology is value-laden, the product of the primordial valuing activities of humankind. It not only arises as technology interacts with political and social factors, but also emerges from the basic fact that technological objects are unique, not universal.

Technological products are particular. They combine specific resources into distinctive entities with unique properties and capabilities. Technological objects embody decisions to develop one kind of knowledge and not another, to use certain resources and not others, to use energy of a specific form and quantity and not some other. There is no purely neutral rationale for all these decisions. Instead, they arise from conceptions of the world related to such issues as permissible uses, good stewardship, and justice.

Contrary to slogans, technological objects do impose on users the way they can be used. Clearly there is latitude in function, but never complete freedom. Advances in medical technology, for example, condition medical practice. A simple tool such as a can opener must be used in a certain way to be effective. Air travel opens up several options but closes others, such as schedule and destination flexibility or the chance simply to stop and enjoy the scenery. The unique entity called the computer embodies specific capabilities and restrictions which homogenize the heterogeneous; it classifies according to its own internal rules. One's available choices are never randomly susceptible to unlimited genius, but depend on the regimen of technology's structure.

The Frankfurt School, from Herbert Marcuse to Jurgen Habermas, has demonstrated compellingly that modern technology, far from being neutral, embodies values incompatible with democracy's core values and operational demands. Martin Heidegger's (1977) seminal essay, "What is Technology," establishes in the existentialist mode that a technological society is at odds with human freedom. And Jacques Ellul (1969a) develops these ruminations into a full-scale critique, demonstrating that technology's efficiency breeds a climate of amorality.

In Ellul's view, industrialized civilizations have their own recognizable "Geist" or characteristic consciousness which he calls *la technique*.

This ethos of efficiency appears everywhere, fully as important to wheat farmers and napalm companies as to communication engineers searching out a channel capacity of one billion bits per second to replace our present 600,000. "Whatever the diversity of countries and methods, they have one characteristic in common: Concern with effectiveness. . . . This is the supreme law which must never be forgotten" (p. x). Ellul exhaustively portrays one thesis: We are so beguiled by machine productivity that we almost unconsciously reconstruct all our social institutions on this model.

Society has entered a new moral posture, designed "to bring human behavior into harmony with the technicized world, to set up a new scale of values in terms of 'la technique' " (Ellul, 1969b, p. 184). Moral values are thus precluded, since *la technique* and judgments about rightness or wrongness are mutually exclusive. *La technique* acts tyrannically as "a spiritual guillotine, decapitating other values, depriving them of social power" (Shriver, 1972, p. 537). A civilization engrossed in means eliminates all moral obstructions to its ascendancy, as "in ancient days men put out the eyes of nightingales in order to make them sing better" (Ellul, 1967, p. 75). Moral judgment lies ruined within the ashes of a meansified civilization. An ethic of efficiency replaces moral goods with averages and probabilities mathematically computed.

Certainly, political and business structures are ravaged by the spirit of machineness, but the situation is doubly ruinous with regard to communications. As the media sketch out one's world, determine one's conversations, and shape one's decisions and self-identity, they foster in the Western soul a technicized view of life. If the burgeoning state and industrial order are *la technique*'s supreme embodiments, our communication systems are its "innermost, and most elusive, manifestation" (Ellul, 1969a, p. xvii). The media are the means to prevent increasing technique "from being felt as too oppressive and to persuade men to submit with good grace" (p. xviii). The devastating invasion of democracy's lifeblood results in people welcoming with enthusiasm the very mechanized constraints which rob them of their freedom. The information system stands powerless with respect to the efficiency motif, but instead subtly adjusts the citizenry to accept it, even to welcome it eagerly. A surfeit of data, far from permitting people to make judgments and form opinions, actually paralyzes them.

Ultimate triumph is sought almost invariably in more streamlined methods, faster computer banks, complex multivariate scales, and electronic consoles of unlimited news and entertainment. Moral purpose is sacrificed to technological excellence. Thus, once the printing press was invented, a process was set in motion for constantly increasing its capacity, speeding its production, and refining it organizationally. Obeying the same autonomous development, electronics is expanded from Atlantic cable to communication satellites, from seven TV channels to thirty, from specialized companies to multi-national conglomerates. And there is a failure to recognize that this self-augmenting process is alien to moral imperatives. Thus the conundrum: Whatever is gained in transmission is lost in ethics. In the process of fabricating expert mechanical systems, the world is sanitized of moral imperatives. Efficiency and morality are polar opposites, in fact, a contradiction in terms.

The stouthearted must hasten to the philosophical trenches. What could normativity possibly mean in an amoral age? Recovering the idea of norms is the catalyst for an authoritative information ethics in a global context. The debate in metaethics over the nature of norms is the open door through which a significant ethics can advance.

In contemporary parlance, one must decenter the concept of normativity; this long way around is the best path home. As Hans Jonas (1984) writes:

> The very same movement which put us in possession of the powers that we now have to be regulated by norms—the movement of modern knowledge called science—has by a necessary complementarity eroded the foundations from which norms are derived; it has destroyed the very idea of norm as such. (p. 22)

This is the conundrum in its starkest terms. Global realities demand global communications. The human race cannot be stitched together effectively by politics or transnational economics. Information is a social necessity for the modern planetary system, but as the system is expanded, its content thickened, and its transmission speeded up, a normative base is being undermined which is needed now more than ever, given the complexities of a global technological civilization. Society is increasingly trapped in Kurt Vonnegut's conundrum: As he reaches into his repertoire of commitments, wisdom, and intelligence, he comes up emptyhanded precisely at the moment he needed them most (Vonnegut, 1952).

In a medieval fable, a dragon is urgently summoned to defend a castle. He pulls together his mighty frame and reaches deep inside for a torrent of fire to scorch the attackers. Nothing happens. The flames in his stomach have died. At the moment of challenge, he becomes little more than a puffing hulk with his fire gone out.

Today, when the demands are most intense, the great information enterprise rouses itself for battle. Ethics committees crop up in professional associations. Alarmists demand more responsible performance. Books and magazines appear on professional virtue, decency, *prime facie* duties, and compassion. The dragon is rumbling, heaving, and puffing—

but the fire has died. At the critical moment, instead of roaring flames, the blaze inside has sputtered out.

Analogously, the long-burning fires of normative thinking are flickering down. At the point where a definitive axiology is most needed for confronting the rage outside, its fundamental inspiration falls away. Principial foundations were designed in a secure Newtonian world with more settled meanings. Now the Enlightenment world view has collapsed, its view of rational being assaulted by Freud and its static universe destroyed by Darwin. The stakes have escalated, the whirlwind is here, and the storm is confronted without a solid theoretical mooring. Obviously, it is foolish to look for a quick fix and unacceptable to hide under fancy rhetoric. But the normativity domain can still be worked as an act of conscience, driven by the need for a vantage point from which to evaluate, judge, and reconstruct all phases of professional morality.

PARADOX

Unfortunately, this dualism and conundrum are exacerbated by a paradox. Norms must be imbedded within culture and history. With this intellectual strategy, transcendental criteria are shifted from a metaphysical, vertical, punctiliar plane to the horizon of community, world, and being; but norms with abiding power they remain, nonetheless. In this view, cultures are sets of symbols that organize the human kingdom and are, therefore, *ipso facto* evaluative. Societies are embodiments of institutions, practices, and structures recognized internally as legitimate. Without allegiance to a web of ordering relations, society becomes inconceivable. A culture's continued existence depends on identifying and defending its normative base. And such a framing of human identity can only be rooted in a proto-norm of universal solidarity. Helmut Peukert (1981) properly insists on universal humanness as the basic principle of ethics and the epicenter of all communication (p. 11).

Refusing to confront normative issues on every level weakens the agenda of universal humanness. How can one legitimately appeal to the supreme value of human life, to an affirmation of unmitigated human dignity, without accepting a network of primal norms—justice, compassion, reciprocity, stewardship—that are nonnegotiable? Everything else comes and goes, both ideologies and the cultures they sustain. If temporality exhausts one's intellectual vistas, wherein lies the possibility of justifying an ethics of human mutuality in the face of anarchy, dialecticism, or equivocation? Without norms that are more than contingent, one cannot finally condemn oppression and dehumanization except on the grounds of personal prejudice or emotional makeup. Absent a defensible conception of the good, praxis will be vitiated by arbitrariness. In fact, without a commitment to norms, an emancipatory intention is radically jeopardized and the byproduct is moral agnosticism. As Basil Mitchell (1980) maintains, the cultural ethos can be decisive without being exclusive. Determinate human beings are not dissolved in a sea of cultural history.

The debate centers, of course, on a philosophy of history. A cultural history with an anthropological bearing predicates an understanding of history in which universals are the problematic and the radically human is epicenter. This is a theory of culture which privileges the human, and in so doing rests on unresolved arguments. If, for example, we maintain one another as humans only in culture, how is it logically possible that humans who themselves are constituted by culture could fully explain the process by which they are enabled to do the explaining? It is an old dilemma in new clothes: Can a theory of something contain itself? As semiotics teaches, there is not the self and language, but one is ultimately inextricable from the other, the first but a manifestation of the second. As one comprehends culture and its catalytic agent, communication, one thereby makes ontological claims about human being.

But that very conundrum contends for history as a normed process. To establish a transformational ethics, it is necessary to articulate an understanding of human being. And any such attribution, no matter how unintended, carries with it one's moral complicity because beingness is conditioned by the language concerning it. Culture encapsulates what humanity values; but undeveloped, that remains only an opening approximation. Universal claims have worked themselves into historical time. No society, as far as is known, has ever declared open hunting season on humans; that is, none exists where three people can be shot during October. All people create life under the presumption of responsibility for those conceived. As a sign of distinctive humanness, one generates symbolic patterns along the boundaries between moral norms and actual behavior, the deepest self and one's collective role, the intentional and the inevitable. There are epiphanal moments suspended outside of oneself, and one can identify them and believe them to be true. The very possibility of universal norms forces a choice among options conducive to universal solidarity. In an ironic twist on conventional skepticism, history as a normed process is not an ancient remnant but the catalyst for conceptual innovation.

The paradox should be evident. In a post-Newtonian, counter-Enlightenment age, norms can only be recovered culturally, can only be situated in history. They are apprehended *in locis*, yet universal proto-norms beyond region and language are essential to maintaining human societies and preventing anti-cultural directions in our indigenous institutions. Master-norms are of the first order, conceptually speaking, yet human beings enter them only through that second-order reality known as ethnicity, geography, and ideology. The first and second orders are distinguished as with a windowpane—knowing there is a decisive break, yet both realms are transparent to each other as well.

In April 1989, the author joined twenty-five others from around the globe in Geneva at the United Nations. The group debated the 1948 Human Rights Declaration—that ingenious appeal to universal human dignity which has survived forty years with surprising resilience. The group worked to solidify it ethically and conceptually for a new worldwide thrust, each group member arrogant enough to speak on behalf of an entire nation.

In October of 1989, in Rizal outside Manila, the author toured a harbor in a small fishing boat, observing how international fisheries had fenced off the productive areas for themselves and destroyed for Filipino subsistence fishermen the meager existence which at least had kept them from starving to death. Through People in Communications, these fishermen were gaining a voice, producing pamphlets, drawing cartoons, holding town meetings, shooting eight-minute videos—hoping to gain a hearing in the capital city where they had no access before. As they presented their case in a small room of a cement-block building, they sounded like the Geneva debates in miniature. The Rizal fishermen appealed for minimal justice; they defied those who did not merely steal their fish but stripped away their rights and dignity. And along the chocolate waters of Rizal Bay rather than the splashing fountains of Geneva, the temporary structure rather than the marble Palace of the Nations, the wooden fishing boats of Asia rather than the chauffeured limousines of Europe, the broken English of October 14 rather than the streamlined electronic translations of April 14, proto-norms were being fashioned incarnate in history.

Yet, without the universal, international mode, there is no opportunity to protect the environment, prevent economic bankruptcy, control dizzying population growth, or reduce the weapons of global destruction. Those who plead for preserving local cultures and those envisioning a global information order are both right. However, these are parallel movements, interconnected in a way that makes folklore from the ground up the *sine qua non* for universal norms rooted in our solidarity as a human race. Thus the paradox: In pursuing high technology as the sinews which bind humanity together, the impassioned need for cultural diversity must be nurtured as well. In the absence of empowering indigenous groups, an elitist, paternalistic system is created at odds with the very social ethics constructed in its name.

At his Guildhall lecture in London in the summer of 1989, Ronald Reagan used the upheaval in China and its vicious repression to celebrate freedom. "You cannot massacre an idea," he said. "You cannot run tanks over hope. You cannot riddle people's yearning with bullets" (Broder, 1989, p. 13).

Mr. Reagan was undoubtedly correct. But he ignored the paradox as he doomed tyranny through the communications revolution. "The biggest of Big Brothers is helpless," he insisted, "against the technology of the information age. Electronic beams blow through the Iron Curtain as if it were lace" (p. 13). But this is not so. Even in open societies, local histories resist intrusion from an anonymous messenger (Broder, 1989). Until symbols resonate from the ground up, the free flow of information remains alien and amorphous. All the sophistication used in negotiating a new world information order between New York City and Mexico City, London and New Delhi, Paris and Caracas, ought to concern itself intraculturally, be it in the villages, between Bangkok and the remote people groups in the mountains, or among a burgeoning ethnic diversity here in the United States.

An assumption of this paper is the elementary distinction between cultural and ethical relativism—the contention that cultural divergence is a source of convergence ethically. The cheerful relativists cannot escape Mannheim's paradox:

> Truth, the relativists say, is culture-bound. But if it were, then they, within their own culture, ought not to see their own culture-bound truth as absolute. They cannot proclaim cultural relativism without rising above it, and they cannot rise above it without giving it up. (Quine, 1975, pp. 327-28)

Dietrich Bonhoeffer (1955), the German ethicist martyred in one of Hitler's concentration camps, challenges the reader to keep his or her penultimate concerns from becoming ultimate. He understood them to be organically unified as a whole, just as the Filipino fisherman's insistence on dignity is a universal truth. Cut loose from the ultimate, penultimate concerns are merely self-serving; substituted for the ultimate domain, they become a strident claim at the expense of another's dignity, a plea for justice now transformed into an abrogation of other moral obligations.

CONCLUSION

Technological civilization is grounded in a duality that often malfunctions. Global media for understanding is in conjugant relationship with instruments of annihilation, the tools for peace themselves solidifying a technological order that makes principial claims alien intruders. This technological order is itself confronted by a conundrum and a paradox, the conundrum being the loss of normativity abetted by the very tools required for any semblance of interconnection on a worldwide scale. Paradoxically, the norms which need recovering are appropriate indigenously but must function universally. Perhaps this duality, conundrum, and paradox can be connected through Ronald Sider's (1979, pp. 203-04) story of Dailyville.

In this story, a small town is surrounded by mountains. A steep and winding highway is its only entrance, and many are injured or die coming down the dangerous road. The good people of the village provide a volunteer ambulance service and maintain an efficient hospital twenty-four hours a day. Then an engineer discovers a likely opening for a short tunnel and everyone applauds the idea. But the local Rockefeller owns a service station along the mountain route, and the mayor has a prosperous restaurant halfway down. Soon, the villagers begin doubting the cost estimates for the new tunnel, and a few harass the idea as too visionary. So, to this day, ambulances continue to scream up the road and medical supplies at the Dailyville hospital are fully stocked. The emergency crews vote badges and honors to one another for a job well done.

A theory of normative ethics proposes to dig a tunnel through the mountain. Instead of bandages and antiseptic on the wounds, structural changes are needed in our world view, fundamental transformations in the way information institutions function. Putting this thesis in its most innocuous form: Substantive advance in information ethics depends on validating the idea of normativity as a necessary though insufficient condition. Discussion of ethics is merely an ideological exercise in the absence of normative criteria. While making norms philosophically unassailable may be impossible, a discourse is needed in which normativity as a minimum becomes *herausforderend*—in Heidegger's terms—pressing itself upon us with compelling force. Only when students of information ethics see normativity as *herausforderend* will the research and writing of information professionals be of enduring significance.

While the profession is busy hammering out more ethical practices and siding with those oppressed or cheated by the system, it must continue to raise a prophetic voice on behalf of the tunnel. Research libraries should be ransacked for the great debates over absolutes, and those serious recent attempts to recover the idea of normativity read, e.g., Hans Jonas' (1984) *The Imperative of Responsibility*, Thomas Nagel's (1986) *View from Nowhere*, Michael Polanyi's (1966) *The Tacit Dimension*, and Frederick Will's (1988) *Beyond Deduction*.

Human reality is structured by ideas. In Heidegger's profound sense, we live in the house of language. Our presuppositions are the grid through which we view the world and act upon it. As we participate in the common task of generating a normative discourse, we contribute to the first-order domain of proto-norms and thereby make possible a meaningful second-order entree to this arena. Providentially, interstices or open spaces still exist in the pointillist canvas called technological civilization. While pure, universal truth is never encountered, attending this territory gives one continuity over space and across time. At least phenomenologically speaking, working on norms enables one to integrate a duality, turn a conundrum into an inspiration, and reconceive a paradox into a mandate for thinking globally while making a difference locally.

REFERENCES

Bonhoeffer, D. (1955). *Ethics*. Translated by N. H. Smith. New York: Macmillan.
Broder, D. (1989, June 19). On technology, tyranny and the Information Age. *Chicago Tribune*, Sec. 1, p. 13.
Buchanan, R. A. (1965). *Technology and social progress*. Oxford: Pergamon Press.
Christians, C. (1989). A theory of normative technology. In E. F. Byrne and J. C. Pitts (Eds.), *Technological transformation: Contextual and conceptual implications* (pp. 123-39). Dordrecht: Kluwer Academic Publishers.
Ellul, J. (1981). *Perspectives on our age*. Translated by J. Neugroschel. New York: Seabury Press.
Ellul, J. (1967). *Presence of the kingdom*. New York: Seabury Press.
Ellul, J. (1969a). *Propaganda*. New York: Alfred A. Knopf.
Ellul, J. (1978). Symbolic function, technology and society. *Journal of Social and Biological Structures, 1*(3), 207-218.
Ellul, J. (1969b). *To will and to do*. Philadelphia: Pilgrim Press.
Fasching, D. J. (n.d.) Theology, technology and transcendence: Reflections on Bernard Lonergan and Jacques Ellul. Unpublished paper, University of South Florida.
Heidegger, M. (1977). What is technology. In W. Lovitt (Trans.), *The question concerning technology, and other essays* (pp. 3-35). New York. Harper & Row.
Jonas, H. (1984). *The imperative of responsibility*. Chicago: University of Chicago Press.
Lancaster, F. W., & Smith, L. C. (Eds.) (in press). *Artificial intelligence and expert systems: Will they change the library?* (Papers presented at the 27th Annual Clinic on Library Applications of Data Processing, 25-27 March 1990). Urbana-Champaign: University of Illinois, Graduate School of Library and Information Science.
McLuhan, M. (1974). At the moment of Sputnik, the planet became a global theatre. *Journal of Communication, 24*(1), 48-58.
Mitchell, B. (1980). *Morality: Religious and secular*. Oxford: Clarendon.
Monsma, S. (Ed.). (1984). *Responsible technology*. Grand Rapids, MI: Eerdmans.
Nagel, T. (1986). *The view from nowhere*. New York: Oxford University Press.
Pacey, A. (1983). *The culture of technology*. Cambridge, MA: The MIT Press.
Peukert, H. (1981). Universal solidarity as goal of communication. *Media Development, 28*(4), 10-12.
Polanyi, M. (1966). *The tacit dimension*. Garden City, NY: Doubleday.
Quine, W. V. (1975). On empirically equivalent systems of the world. *Erkenntnis, 9*(3), 327-328.
Shriver, D. W. (1972). Man and his machines: Four angles of vision. *Technology and Culture, 13*(October), 531-555.

Sider, R. (1979). *Rich Christians in an age of hunger.* Downers Grove, IL: Inter-Varsity Press.

Vonnegut, K. (1952). *Player piano.* New York: Bantam Doubleday Bell Publishing Group.

Will, F. L. (1988). *Beyond deduction: Ampliative aspects of philosophical reflection.* New York: Routledge.

GERALD R. SHIELDS

Assistant Dean (Retired)
School of Information and Library Studies
State University of New York at Buffalo

The FBI Creates An Awareness of Librarian Ethics: An Opinionated Historical Review

INTRODUCTION

Paula Kaufman, Director of Academic Information Services Group for Columbia University, became the whistleblower on what is now known to be one of several visits made by agents of the Federal Bureau of Investigation to libraries seeking information on the use of that institution by "foreigners." She notified the New York Library Association's Intellectual Freedom Committee Chair that the Math/Science Library at Columbia had been the target of a visit by two agents asking a clerical employee about foreigners in the library. Included in her report was the startling intelligence that in a subsequent visit with the agents, she was told that their activities were part of an FBI Library Awareness Program. All they were seeking, they said, was that librarians be alert to use of their libraries by people from countries "hostile to the U. S., such as the Soviet Union" and to report their observations to the FBI's New York City office (Kaufman, 1988).

It is noteworthy that Ms. Kaufman made it clear to the agents that it was institutional policy that such surveillance of users was unprofessional, particularly in a collection that had no classified materials. Undoubtedly, it was her personal sense of professionalism that led her to report the incident rather than ignore it, as was likely the case in some other area research libraries. ALA, upon learning of the incident, contacted John Otto, then acting director of the FBI, requesting information on the program called, by the New York office, "Library Awareness." NYLA wrote to the New York City FBI office and received

19

a letter that acknowledged receipt and promised to get back with an answer.

ALA received an answer from Milt Ahlerich, Acting Assistant Director, admitting that such a program existed. He made it sound as if the activity was restricted to the New York office because they wanted to alert librarians to this potential danger that "members of hostile countries or their agents attempting to gain access to information that could be potentially harmful to our national security." He stated that they were seeking "assistance" (McFadden, 1987, p. B2).

The NYLA inquiry resulted in a letter from Mr. Otto making the same admission and agreeing that the New York FBI officers would be contacting the Association with more information. After six weeks of silence, Dr. Helen F. Flowers, president of NYLA, and Nancy Lian, the executive director for NYLA, met with Robert D. McFadden and turned over copies of their correspondence to him. On September 18, 1987, *The New York Times* broke the story on the front page under McFadden's byline. He got an admission from the New York City office that "fewer" than twenty libraries had been contacted. They refused to confirm that any such contacts had been made outside the metropolitan area. James Fox, deputy assistant director of the New York office of the FBI, is quoted as insisting that "hostile intelligence has had some success working the campuses and libraries, and we are going around telling people what to be alert for . . . we don't want librarians to become amateur sleuths" (p. B2).

It is important to note at this point that the FBI has gone to considerable lengths to avoid making much in the way of written statements about their activities, preferring to make telephone statements or appearance behind closed doors. At no time have they substantiated the majority of their allegations. For instance, it was at the time of the *Times* story and the subsequent pick-up by the wire services that Anne Heanue, associate director of the ALA Washington office, had the following response read to her:

> The FBI is responsible for countering the intelligence gathering efforts of hostile foreign intelligence services. The damage being done to our country by such foreign intelligence services is substantial. The FBI's foreign counterintelligence investigative efforts encompass a variety of approaches, all of which are within U. S. Attorney General guidelines and United States laws.
>
> The FBI has documented instances, for more than a decade, of hostile intelligence officers who have exploited libraries by stealing proprietary, sensitive, and other information and attempting to identify and recruit American and foreign students in American libraries. The FBI, therefore, in an effort to thwart this activity is endeavoring,

on a limited basis, to educate knowledgeable individuals in specialized libraries to this hostile intelligence threat.

The FBI has historically depended upon the American public's assistance in carrying out its investigative responsibilities. The FBI has absolutely no interest in interfering with the American public's academic freedoms or First Amendment rights. (ALA Intellectual Freedom Committee, 1987, pp. 241-43)

This release documents the cynicism with which the FBI operates. It has been no secret that the current administration is carrying on the policy designed to limit access to information in commercial databases that bear sensitive government data. There has been a constant pressure, reported assiduously in countless releases by the ALA Washington office, by the government to get publishers to monitor the people using their systems and to seek limits to access to those databases. And in the revelations of the Awareness Program it is obvious that, having met resistance from publishers, the government has been trying to pressure academic and research libraries to do the same by disclosing user names and the subjects of the searches to the FBI.

In all of the subsequent investigations and meetings with the legislative committees, NCLIS, and ALA, the Bureau has not once revealed that it has sought information on specific individuals known to be engaged in terrorist activities, nor has it offered any information that links such database searches by individuals to such activities. It has been clearly established by the U. S. Supreme Court that foreign nationals residing in the U. S. enjoy the same First Amendment protection as do its citizens. They also as aliens are equally protected by the due process stipulations of the Fifth Amendment and the equal protection clause of the Fourteenth Amendment.

Such veiled hints that the expulsion of Soviet employee Gennadiy F. Zakharov was triggered by his recruitment of a Queens College student he met in the library have proven to be false. In fact, another student employed at the U. N. gave the name of the Queens student to the Soviet agent after having seen it on a Queens College bulletin board soliciting library research services, according to recent research by Simmons doctoral student Cheryl Ann McHenry (1989). Such blatant manipulation of the facts by the FBI seems to point to mere justification for a "fishing expedition" and a cynical awareness that the very idea planted in the public mind that the FBI is watching the use of libraries by individuals will have a chilling effect which can help accomplish a reduction in the use of scientific and technical information.

The people gathered together at this conference are here to try and determine if it is within their power to inspire a righting of these wrongs, if there is something in their calling as librarians that can inspire them to action.

Developing a Professional Code of Ethics

Ethics for librarians have been a struggle for a long time. Codes were adopted and proposed for revision. In 1903, Mary W. Plumer authored one; in 1922, Charles Knowles Bolton managed to get a revision passed by ALA; in 1929, uneasiness with the document surfaced with a proposed code that languished and never saw ratification. These codes were primarily an extended listing of commandments one might expect from a summit meeting of administrators, e.g., thou shalt not covet thy neighbor library's budget, thou shalt not speak ill of thy administrator, thou shalt wear sensible shoes, etc.

From 1968 to 1981 there was a constant struggle to present a code that would be adopted by the ALA Council. During this period was developed the concept that libraries as institutions must find and defend methods for people to find what they want to know in use of the graphic record. Almost immediately, a moral tenet was attached to the library's right to promulgate the right to know. Librarians have been finding ways of saying just that and insisting that to deny such access is a moral and ethical blasphemy against the U. S. Bill of Rights.

In making the statement now known as the Library Bill of Rights, librarians began to learn that when information storage and retrieval systems are manipulated so as to discourage or prevent untrammeled and intimidation-free inquiry, there is a cause and effect. Minds begin to wither, knowledge retreats, and a self-protective silence ensues.

Admittedly, for some librarians there is still an uneasiness connected to embracing the burden of advocacy of the right of free access to information. Advocacy has its roots in the Latin word *vocalis,* meaning to voice, or break the silence. And it is against societal norms to bring attention upon oneself by breaking silence and embracing advocacy.

At the ALA Convention in 1981, a revision of a Code of Professional Ethics was adopted. It is a succinct document, advisory and moralistic in its exhortations for professional conduct. There are six paragraphs in it; however, it is in the third paragraph, wherein librarians are called upon to "protect each user's right to privacy with respect to information sought or received, and materials consulted, borrowed or acquired" (ALA Council, 1982), that the true brunt of the ethics of librarianship is placed.

Careful inspection will reveal that the Library Bill of Rights stands as a separate document from the Code of Professional Ethics. The former is an advisory policy statement aimed at the institution of the library. The latter is a statement of professional aspirations and conditions aimed at those individuals who would practice librarianship. So it is that librarians have worked with a document for nearly fifty years that has been aimed primarily at institutions. On the other hand, the Code of Professional Ethics has languished in a revisionist limbo for decades and only recently resurfaced as a statement of policy for the individual.

Unfortunately, when the code was adopted in May 1981, there is no evidence that even one cork was popped or one fiddle bowed. No one seemed to really care or even be aware of the document. For a while, it looked as if its only contribution to the profession was to have supplied some librarians with an excuse to extract support funds from their institution to attend ALA committee meetings.

Certainly, this lethargy was not because there were no moral or ethical dilemmas flaring up almost daily. Legitimate and illegitimate authorities have been constantly after the library to violate the rights of those who come to it for access free from intimidation and with respect for the right to privacy. It is just that the issues have been primarily fought at the institutional level, with the librarian as agent.

It has long been recognized that, in some cases, librarians were being either punished or intimidated where they tried to defend the library's institutional stand on intellectual freedom matters. The ALA Office for Intellectual Freedom has conducted a fairly long campaign to promote the adoption of state statutes that would provide some legal basis for the protection of records identifying the patron with the materials used. To date, only eleven states have failed to adopt such a statute. This push for statutory protection was in recognition of the need to shield the librarian in order to accomplish the stated goals of the institution.

ETHICAL RESPONSIBILITY VS. PATRIOTIC DUTY

When the nation's media focused upon the librarian as guardian of the right to privacy in the retrieval of information from the libraries and databanks, it was fascinating news imagery: the librarian up against one of the more intimidating federal agencies, the FBI.

When the Library Awareness Program came to light, librarians found themselves the objects of admiration for their professional stand against intimidation of themselves and the users of libraries. Headlines delighted in pointing out that the librarians were refusing to act as spies. The FBI not only precipitated this public relations coup for librarians, they also compounded it by making false and misleading statements about their program. For example, early on the FBI claimed

that it was only in and around New York that the program was active.
The following table is a list of documented visits reported by ALA as
of May 10, 1988 (ALA Intellectual Freedom Committee, 1988):

TABLE 1
ALA-REPORTED LIBRARY VISITS BY FBI

Institution	Library	Contact
ACADEMIC LIBRARIES		
Columbia	Math/Science Library	Paula Kaufman
N.Y. University	Courant Institute of Mathematical Science	Nancy Gubman
University of Maryland	Engineering/Physical Sciences Library	Herb Foerstel
George Mason University		Charlene Hurt
University of Kansas	(details unavailable)	
University of California at Los Angeles	Engineering/Math Science Library	Ruth B. Gibbs
Pennsylvania State University	University Libraries	James G. Neal
University of Michigan	Engineering/ Transportation Library	Maurita Peterson Holland
University of Houston		Scott Chafin, University Counselor
University of Cincinnati		Dorothy Byers
University of Wisconsin at Madison		Alexander Rolich
University of Utah	Government Documents Library	Roger K. Hanson
*State University of N.Y. at Buffalo	Lockwood Library	Stephen Roberts
PUBLIC LIBRARIES		
Broward Cty (Fl) System		Selma Algaze
Brooklyn		Ellen Rudley
New York City		Paul Fasana
OTHER CONTACTS		
Information Industry Association		Ken Allen

*At Buffalo, a specific request was made, citing a specific individual, and was followed
by presentation of the required subpoena.

Following are some of the allegations made by the FBI as to the
extent with which libraries are being used by the Soviet Intelligence

Services (SIS). In a report entitled *The KGB and the Library Target, 1962-Present*, prepared by the Intelligence Division of the FBI and dated January 1, 1988, FBI Director William S. Sessions contended that:

> Included as an element of Soviet Exchange Student tasking has been the identification of scientific-technical libraries; systems of their work; possibilities for subscribing to literature and reports from the libraries or other institutions of learning; qualifications and specialties of students being trained and where they are placed after graduation from a university or college, and with which government institutions' regular business connections were being maintained.
>
> The SIS has utilized clandestine means to obtain large volumes of documents from the Special Libraries Association (SLA).
>
> Officials in Moscow have instructed SIS officers to obtain from the Library of Congress various types of information through the use of SIS sources.
>
> The SIS has been known to target specific librarians to be considered as possible contacts for agent development. Background investigations on these librarians, and if necessary, physical surveillance of them, have been encouraged. The SIS has obtained the *Biographical Directory of American and Canadian Librarians* and can utilize this document to identify specific librarians for targeting. (FBI Intelligence, 1988, pp. 16-17)

The report is a lengthy series of allegations, including claims to having documented cases of librarians having been recruited out of public libraries and encouraged to seek positions in more attractive targets. The report alleges that the SIS has perpetrated large scale theft of microfiche, but strangely, it does not claim to have documented such activity as being part of the Soviet intelligence gathering program.

The largest part of the report is comprised of excerpts from the April, 1987 issue of *New York Magazine* which reported on Gennadiy F. Zakharov's activities with the Queens student who was never contacted in the library. It concludes by contending that librarians are being asked to report on foreign agent activity as a patriotic duty and that in no way are they being asked to compromise the rights of the citizens using the libraries.

Librarian as Guardian of Free Access

Looking back over the editorial comments from various media on the librarian's reaction to the FBI visits, one finds a tone of respect not always evident in such accounts. It is impressive to hear politicians, writers, researchers and other opinion-makers talking about the librarian as a guardian of the free and democratic access to libraries for all people.

Is this to the benefit of the profession? Samuel Rothstein (1968), while discussing the hope for professionalization of librarianship, said that "like any professional group (they) need some kind of statement which will indicate what they are and what they stand for" (p. 157).

Librarians have been prepared through their exposure to the Library Bill of Rights to offer guidance and assistance to the client who comes to them for help; but they have always tried to make the distinction that such assistance was not to be an attempt to make moral and ethical judgments about the individual and his or her motives for seeking information.

Louis Ranlett (1939) discussed the librarian's ethics and sounded most contemporary when he said that "public confidence in our discretion and approachability is more important than a reputation of always being right. The latter ought to keep people at arm's length. The former will permit them to speak to us without whispering" (p. 740).

Most librarians tend to avoid taking sides or entering into conflicts, perhaps out of pride that what they do benefits others. At the same time, many librarians have difficulty in maintaining their highly touted neutrality when information is being requested by those who may be perceived as somehow unsuitable.

Society's real concern for protecting itself from violence and criminal activity can and will make claims upon librarians from time to time. In order for the librarian to make an assessment of the particular circumstances, there will be a constant necessity for evaluating those stated ethics and seeking more revealing parables and homilies that can reduce the tendency to panic during a situation of moral stress and ethical dilemma.

The FBI Library Awareness Program is a compelling reason for all of the profession to take a good look at not only their own but also at the federal government's roles in pushing the librarian toward a confrontation over ethics. The damage caused by the number of government documents being removed from public access, some with and others without a security classification, is well known. The arguments publicly made by the FBI for their library contacts seem to be based upon a misunderstanding of the scientific communication process and the purpose of libraries in the growth of knowledge. Dr. Sessions in his statement to Congress allowed that "it is the very lacking of information and idea exchanges in a closed society that stifles creativity, suppresses the imagination, and acts as a barrier to social, economic progress" (FBI Intelligence, p. 32). Yet the Bureau would have librarians try to selectively create a "closed society" within our own.

Another irony is all the activity that deplores the foreign nationals from having access to unclassified information, particularly when it falls into the hands of communist countries. Yet many of the databases being turned over to the private sector corporations are in reality multinational in ownership, owing allegiance to no political group and often head-quartered in such places as France, Belgium, Japan, and Germany. Examples have already appeared wherein some of those agencies handling U. S.-inspired databases deal directly with some of the communist-block nations and other political entities such as Iran.

INFORMATION AND THE POWER STRUCTURE

Looking beyond the rhetoric and the posturing that has particularized the FBI Library Awareness Program, an agenda begins to surface. In this age of technology, it is not the minerals, water power, fossil fuels, etc., that are going to serve society; it is information that is the infinite resource humankind has left. Information collection, storage, and retrieval are essential to the survival of society when the finite resources are no longer available.

At the same time, it is difficult to put a fence around information, to bury it underground, to push it through a pipeline, or to harness it to the wheel. However, information in the hands of a few will create the new elite, the power structure able to dominate the remainder of society much in the manner that those who control the mineral and real estate resources today do.

Given that the FBI admits that this sort of activity has been going on for at least a decade, and that in the past eight years an accelerating program seeking control of all information has been promoted at the highest government levels, one realizes that this is the true national information policy.

In his report to the ALA Council in January 1989, James Schmidt revealed how strong the drive is among those with vested interest in controlling access, and that this drive is based on the construction of a climate of intimidation and fear. At its previous annual conference, ALA had endorsed the passage of H.R.4947 and S.2361, intended to give federal protection from disclosure of personally identifiable information about library users as kept by libraries. However, by October 1988, ALA was forced to agree to withdraw the library portion of that legislation because it was well known that an amendment was in the works that would have replaced the court order requirement for access to such information with a simple letter from the FBI (or other government agency) stating that such inquiry was a matter of national security; it would have imposed a gag order on any library employee who had been questioned by an agent of the government about library patrons; and it would have subordinated all state statutes protecting such records when it was a matter of national security. The bill, without a mention of libraries other than those maintained by video rental agencies, was passed. Thus, one cannot find out what videos one's legislator is renting, but one can find out what materials he or she is checking out at the library!

Negative publicity has not given the FBI pause. Director Sessions repeated his promise to continue to visit libraries.

> The librarians . . . may have reason to contact the FBI regarding an individual if he identifies himself as a Soviet national and:
> 1) [seeks] assistance in conducting research in the library;
> 2) requests a librarian to refer him to a student or professor who might assist him in a research project;
> 3) advises a librarian that he is conducting research for an unnamed Soviet friend and needs access to specific documents;
> 4) [removes materials] without properly checking them out of the library; and
> 5) asks a librarian . . . for biographical or personality assessment information . . . on a student or academician. (FBI Intelligence, pp. 9-10)

Sessions goes on to say that the FBI also wants to know about anyone who says they are doing some project for Soviet-bloc nationals. He states that the FBI does not want to hear about anyone who does not fit the above criteria. He claims that the FBI will not force librarians to comply or give information, but he feels certain that once everything is explained to them, librarians will be happy to assist.

To many observers, it is clear that the FBI program is part of a systematic, coordinated, interagency effort to prevent access to unclassified information, and that the coordination emanates from a multi-agency Technology Transfer Intelligence Committee hosted by the CIA. The committee has reported their concern over the issue of sensitive but unclassified information. There seems to be no hesitancy on their part to use whatever intimidation or coercion they can muster to create a climate of fear and mistrust. There seems to be a tacit admission that surveillance by government agencies, many of them shrouded in secrecy and covert activities, is an acceptable way to run a democracy.

CONCLUSION

An ideal has haunted humans for centuries, a hope that somehow, through perseverance, a world can be created without fear and without hunger, where justice is commonplace and peace can become a reality. Librarians have only recently discovered their real and measurable role in maintaining that ideal, and can take solace from a man who half a century ago captured the imagination of this nation with his dream of

One World. "Freedom," Wendell L. Wilkie said, "is an indivisible word. If we want to enjoy it, and fight for it, we must be prepared to extend it to everyone, whether they be rich or poor, whether they agree with us or not, no matter what their race or color of their skin" (Bartlett, 1980, p. 824).

Libraries have always been based upon an optimistic view of the future. There are many librarians who have already committed themselves to "each user's right to privacy with respect to information sought or received, and materials consulted, borrowed or acquired." Those librarians who have not despaired offer hope to all for the future.

REFERENCES

ALA Council. (1982). Statement on professional ethics (latest revision of Code of Ethics). *American Libraries* (October), 595 (reprint of 1981 statement).

ALA Intellectual Freedom Committee. (1988). *FBI Library Awareness Program.* ALA Council Document No. 41.1. Chicago: American Library Association.

ALA Intellectual Freedom Committee advises librarians on the FBI Library Awareness Program. (1987). *Newsletter on Intellectual Freedom, 36*(6), 241-243.

Bartlett, J. (1980). *Familiar quotations: A collection of passages, phrases, and proverbs traced to their sources in ancient and modern times* (15th and 125th anniversary ed., rev. and enl.). E. M. Beck (Ed.). Boston: Little, Brown.

FBI Intelligence Division. (1988). *The KGB and the library target, 1962-present.* Washington, DC: USGPO.

Kaufman, P. T. (1988). Statement to the House Subcommittee on Civil and Constitutional Rights. In *FBI counterintelligence visits to libraries* (pp. 74-83). Washington, DC: USGPO.

McFadden, R. D. (1987, September 18). FBI in New York asks librarians' aid in reporting on spies. *The New York Times,* p. A1.

Ranlett, L. F. (1939). The librarians have a word for it: Ethics. *Library Journal, 64*(22), 738-740.

Rothstein, S. (1968). In search of ourselves. *Library Journal, 93*(2), 156-157.

SELECTED BIBLIOGRAPHY

The following list was drawn from "The Confidentiality of Library Records: Articles, Cases and Statutes" with the kind permission of the compiler Lisa L. Satterlund, University of Bridgeport Law Library, Bridgeport, Connecticut.

Berry, J. (1988). Should librarians support NCLIS? (Editorial). *Library Journal, 113*(6), 6.

Berry, J. (1988). Where was NCLIS? (Editorial). *Library Journal, 113*(13), 4.

Brown v. Johnston, 328 N.W. 2d 510 (Iowa). 463 U.S. 1208 (1983). (Constitutional right of privacy overridden by state's interest in criminal charges.)

California v. Greenwood, 108 S. Ct. 1625 (1988). (Ruled that privacy right does not exist unless society says it is reasonable.)

The constitutional right to confidentiality. (1982). *George Washington Law Review, 51,* 133-144.

DeCandido, G. A. (1988). FBI presents Library Awareness to NCLIS at closed meeting. *Library Journal, 113*(7), 16.

Evidentiary use of a criminal defendant's reading habits and political conversations: United States v. Giese. (1979). *Harvard Law Review, 93,* 419.

FBI accuses Soviets of spying at libraries. (1988, May 19). *The New York Times*, p. B11.
FBI counterintelligence visits to libraries: Hearings before the Subcommittee on Civil and Constitutional Rights of the House Committee on the Judiciary. 100th Congress, 2nd Session (June 20 and July 13, 1988). Washington, DC: USGPO.
Foerstel, H. N. (1988). Statement to the House Subcommittee on Civil and Constitutional Rights. *FBI counterintelligence visits to libraries* (pp. 84-90). Washington, DC: USGPO.
Greenhouse, L. (1988, July 14). FBI defends library monitoring program. *The New York Times*, p. A17.
Griswald V. Connecticut, 381 U.S. 479 (1965). (The First Amendment includes freedom of inquiry and freedom to learn.)
Isbell, M. K., & Cook, M. K. (1986). Confidentiality of online bibliographic searches: Attitudes and practices. *RQ, 25*(4), 483-487.
Kleindienst v. Mandel, 408 U.S. 753 (1971). (The First Amendment includes the right to receive information and ideas.)
Linowes, D. F., & Hoyman, M. M. (1982). Data confidentiality: Social research and the government. *Library Trends, 30*(3), 489-503.
McHenry, C. A. (1989). *The FBI Library Awareness Program and foreign counterintelligence visits to libraries: A content analysis of source documents.* Unpublished doctoral dissertation, Simmons College, Boston, MA.
O'Neil, R. M. (1973). Libraries, librarians and the First Amendment. *University of Cincinnati Law Review, 42*, 209-252.
Parrish v. Civil Service Commission, 66 Cal. Reports 2d 260, 425 F. 2d 223, and 57 California Reporter 623 (1967). (The county cannot compel worker to violate the privacy of third parties.)
Robins, N. (1988). Spying in the stacks: The FBI's invasion of the libraries. *The Nation, 481*(April 9), 498-502.
Thefts of patent information puzzle university librarians. (1989, August 21). *The New York Times*, p. A11.
United States v. Rumely, 345 U.S. 41 (1953). (Congressional committee denied access to list of purchasers of certain books.)
Virginia State Board of Pharmacy v. Virginia Citizens Consumer Council, 425 U.S. 748 (1976). (Society has strong interests in the free flow of information.)
Wilson, M. K. (1981). Surveillance of individual reading habits: Constitutional limitation of disclosure of library borrower lists. *American University Law Review, 30*(1), 275-321.

HERBERT S. WHITE

Professor and former Dean
School of Library and Information Science
Indiana University
Bloomington, Indiana

Teaching Professional Ethics to Students of Library and Information Science

INTRODUCTION

Discussions of ethics have been around for hundreds, indeed thousands, of years, and have recently received considerable new attention in the library profession. The author's late friend and colleague Manfred Kochen (1987) offered a very useful analysis in which he attempted to track the development of ethics, which over time many people have claimed as their own domain, but with regard to which there remains a great deal of confusion. The author's own attempt to spotlight the lack of consistency in the library field, as librarians seek not only to define but also to claim ethics as something they possess and others fail to honor, can be inferred from the working title of an upcoming *Library Journal* article column, "My Truths Are More Moral Than Your Biases" (White, 1990). Kochen's article notes that ethics deal with principles for judging right and wrong. That sounds self-evident enough, but what is right? Who is right? Machiavelli had no difficulty with the issue because to him, might made right. Eighteenth-century theologians postulated that ethical behavior was behavior in accordance with the will of God, but to recognize the difficulty with that definition it need only be remembered that most religious persecution, including the Inquisition and the death warrant for Salman Rushdie, was and is ostensibly in the name of God, and burning at the stake was justified quite neatly on the premise that God would not let an innocent person burn to death. Since they all did burn, they were also declared guilty of heresy, or whatever they were charged with. William James helped us along by noting that

31

it was the duty of man to know the will of God and keep it (easily said!).
John Stuart Mill postulated that right is that which produces human
happiness, while Immanuel Kant equated right with reason. Of course,
today it is commonly known what difficulties can be found in work
settings with the word *reasonable*. "Be reasonable" often means that the
speaker is being reasonable while the person who is being spoken to is
not. The search for compromise as a reasonable solution runs contrary
to the general belief that right equals reasonable and only the unrea-
sonable need compromise (thereby giving a new meaning to the term.)
To add to the confusion, one is also urged to stand by one's principles
and never compromise them away. Nietzsche pragmatically argued that
by *right* was meant that which produced the next stage of evolution,
what Nietzsche called the *superman*. That makes ethics easy to define
for oneself, because ethics then becomes whatever one wants it to be,
from conclusions one has already reached. One need only note what
Hitler was able to do with an extension of Nietzsche's philosophy.

THE COMPLEXITY OF ETHICAL CONCERNS

However, this is not a paper on historical developments of ethics,
better left to individuals far better qualified than the author. Suffice to
say that the confusion and difficulty surrounding the topic continues to
this day. When newsman Bill Moyers (1989) conducts an in-depth
interview with modern-day ethicist Michael Josephson, many pages of
eloquent exposition in conversation with one of the brightest interviewers
of the day nevertheless leaves one with the impression that Josephson
is dealing with interpretations of the golden rule — "Do unto others as
you would have them do unto you." It is certainly a useful and valid
statement, but it does not really help in more than a very limited sense,
e.g., do not murder or do not steal. But does not a librarian give
information to individuals who would do with it what the librarian
would not? That does not fit nearly as well, and it spotlights the problem
that ethical concerns for professionals are not easy and obvious issues.
Librarians oppose censorship, but the Library Bill of Rights and the
codes of ethics adopted by various American Library Association bodies
really state the obvious and solve no problems. Library schools must
indeed teach this, but more importantly, they must teach how to make
it work. However, professional conflicts fall on more complicated ground.
What are librarians' responsibilities to employers, be they corporations,
universities, or public agencies? Can these responsibilities be contradictory to those owed to library users? What if the inadequacy of funding
or staffing provided by library funding agencies means that librarians

are providing inadequate service to them? It is a fascinating characteristic of the professional library literature that librarians worry a great deal about whether or not government documents should be released to the public through the depository library system, and not one whit whether or not anybody can find them in a massive cataloging backlog, assuming the documents are cataloged at all. What is the professional ethical concern in a cataloging backlog; or in a failure to have adequate reference service available; or in the recognition that, while a copy of a book has been purchased, the patron cannot have it because it is charged out and the librarian refuses to borrow another copy? One can see that the issues involving professional ethics are more complicated than they first appear.

Employer-Employee Conflicts

The conflicts between responsibility to the profession and to the employer have been discussed in many fields. In general, it has been noted that humanists, such as history or philosophy professors, see their responsibility to their profession, and their employer and his or her value systems play only an incidental role. By contrast, scientists and engineers are seen to owe their greater allegiances to their employer, and they do what the employer asks them to do. Thus, when the author came to Oak Ridge, Tennessee in 1953, there were many individuals there who had worked hard and long on the development of the atomic bomb in the early 1940s. They found out only after Hiroshima and Nagasaki that they had been working on a destructive bomb. It is an interesting sidelight of ethical history to know that some of the refugee scientists from Germany who did know were perfectly willing to drop the bomb on Germany, but after the Germans had already surrendered in the spring of 1945, these scientists were reluctant to drop it on the Japanese, whom they saw as a lesser enemy not deserving of impersonal annihilation. Other individuals, of course, fought the Japanese with far more enthusiasm than they could muster for fighting the Germans. That is, of course, blatant racism, and totally unacceptable even if still practiced in 1991, but quite acceptable in 1942 if one remembers the totally illegal (as well as unnecessary) Nisei internment. What is the role of ethics if it is bent to personal and convenient value systems? Is it wrong to block the entrance to an abortion clinic but acceptable to block the entrance to a nuclear power plant? Do library educators need to deal with these issues?

One company that attempts to straddle the issues of public image when it comes to ethics is Dow Chemical. Dow was one of the developers of Agent Orange as used in Vietnam, in response to the perceived government need for a defoliant. It is clear that Dow is now sensitive to implications it had no particular reasons to anticipate, and certainly any chemical contractor could have produced this product whose chemical formula was known. However, Dow is now recruiting young people who want to find "chemical solutions to societal problems." Dow's primary objective, now as then, is to its stockholders, who expect it to make a profit; certainly, the president of Dow knows this—and the young Dow chemist will learn it. Bankrupt ethical organizations are not much good to anybody, and the difficulty is in maintaining a balance. It is sometimes not easy. Exxon is now roundly condemned for allowing the Alaska oil spill to take place, but that oil spill was probably caused by an Exxon employee who was a long-time substance abuser, and some of the people who now condemn Exxon are the same ones who would have objected if Exxon had put into place a tough program of mandatory or random drug testing, and fired the offenders. Some of those people who would prefer to have it both ways are librarians, and some even serve on the ALA Council. The problems of human imbalance are not new, and technology at least offers the potential for greater distribution. In libraries, it means enhanced bibliographic access and document delivery which might help a doctor in a backward area. In earthquakes, the loss of life in California was far smaller than in Armenia, despite the fact that California's was a quake of greater magnitude, because building construction technology in the United States is better and leaves far fewer homeless.

PERSONAL ETHICS VS. PROFESSIONAL RESPONSIBILITIES

Private citizens have responsibilities to prevent injustice, evil, racial hatred, nuclear holocaust, and environmental blight; they are also free to develop personal interpretations. What happens when personal standards get in the way of assigned professional duties as subordinate employees and, just perhaps, in the way of professional ethics? It is, as with the Exxon case, always easy to judge with 20/20 hindsight. German scientists should have refused to develop the poison gases used in Auschwitz and the other death camps, and Werner von Braun was a "bad" German when he helped develop the V-2 bomb that fell indiscriminately all over London. Later, of course, he became a "good" German, and finally the quality of Germans was irrelevant and the Russians were "bad." Now that the Russians are getting to be "good," Americans are in danger of having only the "bad" South Africans, and there are not enough of them to go around.

Retrospective judgments are always applied by winners to losers.

Thus, the Andersonville Trial occurred because Andersonville was a Confederate prison, while what happened in the Union prison at Elmira, New York was irrelevant because the North won the war. Those who have seen the play *The Andersonville Trial* (Levitt, 1960) will recall the idealistic young prosecutor who is ultimately brought into line by the military judges who understand that they are not here in a search for justice or ethics, but rather to find Captain Wirtz guilty so that he can be hung. There are those who are rhapsodic about the Nuremberg trials, but this author has his difficulties. Countries are still using poison gas and tactics of starvation on their own citizens, and the world does not even seem to notice. Indeed, representatives of these countries participate in UN symposia that extol human rights.

In any case, professionals have their ethical codes that can get in the way of practice. Thus, the Hippocratic Oath would require any Jewish surgeon to have attempted to save the life of Adolph Hitler. Lawyers are supposed to do their best to defend their client even if they are certain he or she is guilty, and if possible get their client freed on a technicality even if that outcome means that more crimes will be committed. A recent graduation speech on ethical conduct was delivered at the Wharton School of the University of Pennsylvania by an investment banker who clearly does have a social conscience as well as a knack for making money, Felix Rohatyn. He noted the emphasis in American business on making money through junk bonds, leveraged buyouts, green mail, and golden parachutes, and urged these new graduates to go out and not simply manipulate blips on a computer screen but build the country. Rohatyn's audience of future financiers cheered him, but what impact his talk had will not be known until much later. It is significant that Rohatyn said what he did because he thought that the Wharton professors had not said it, and later interviews with the audience of graduates indicate that his assumption was correct. What the professors had been teaching is what the financial community had wanted them to teach; by extension, that included leveraged buyouts and junk bonds.

What Library Schools Teach

What is taught in library schools, and what does the profession want to be taught there? Yehoshua Bar-Hillel, in a talk presented at a conference in Aberystwyth, Wales, stated quite simply that the job of librarians and information specialists was to help their patrons find whatever information they needed. What those people did with that information was not the librarian's concern. It is certainly a simple ethic if it can be adopted, and it has similarities to what doctors and lawyers are supposed to believe. However, Bar-Hillel's thesis opens the door to a great deal of second-guessing. It also contradicts the mood of many individuals who come to library school to become librarians because they want to make the world better. Rohatyn would not have had to make his speech at a library school graduation since library students are not really in their chosen profession for the money.

The big ethical issue for librarians, in their professional literature and in their educational emphasis, has been on access to information. It is an important issue, and it concentrates on familiar themes. Unfettered access is championed and strong stands are taken against government policies that attempt to withhold information either through restrictions on distribution that affect depository systems or by attempting to limit distribution by pseudo-security classifications such as unclassified but sensitive or by charging for government information. Government attempts to limit access have been effectively and articulately opposed. The most significant and visible impact is in the fight against censorship and the banning of books, although banning usually applies only to removal after purchase. Attempts to remove such material as the work of Judy Blume or Kurt Vonnegut on the grounds of unsuitability, or the diary of Anne Frank because it is "depressing" have been vigorously opposed. There are also fights, some equally vehement and some less so, against censorship from the "good" side— individuals who consider *Huckleberry Finn* or *Little Black Sambo* as racist, or works such at *The Taming of the Shrew* as sexist. This is always a difficulty with classics. Shakespeare would not have thought *The Merchant of Venice* blatantly anti-Semitic but simply the normal thought of the time among Shakespeare's countrymen.

In any case, librarians fight these issues with a will, even to the extent of finding themselves allied with child pornographers, because the ALA Office of Intellectual Freedom believes, and many agree, that nothing should be censored. In general, there is no difficulty in getting students to accept these concepts. Many come from library backgrounds, and their value systems are already inclined to accept the premise of open access.

The Book Selection Process and *De Facto* Censorship

It has already been noted that censorship in libraries consists primarily of removing material already purchased. Below the surface are other issues not as readily addressed. The decision not to buy something in the first place is more easily defended as long as the claim is that this is not censorship but merely the implementation of value judgments, since obviously not every item can be purchased. If there are librarian biases in this process, it is a thicket into which lawyers would have difficulty following unless librarians were foolish enough to put some of these things in writing. Do librarians discriminate in their own decisions? Perhaps not blatantly, but it is human nature to consider the things one agrees with as more important and worthwhile than the things one disagrees with. Librarians have very little latitude in some areas, but in the decisions of what to buy and what not to buy, they have a great deal. Students are urged in library school courses to purchase "quality" books, but how is that judgment to be made? A study by Indiana University professor Judith Serebnick (1981) notes that librarians buy books that are reviewed, whether or not the reviews are favorable, in preference to books that are not reviewed. Critics who argue that libraries fail to purchase material published by alternative presses may be stressing the wrong point. They argue that libraries must acquire such alternative publications dealing with "different" lifestyles as a public service, while others would take the Baltimore County view that libraries should buy books that users want to read. That is an important issue of distinction, and it does get discussed in some major library education courses.

The reason librarians fail to purchase alternative books is neither an ethical nor a reader-oriented value judgment. The reason they are not bought is because selecting them is too much trouble. Does the library have a role in persuading to a "correct" point of view through selection policies on such issues as nuclear disarmament, freedom of choice for abortion, or the equal rights amendment? Librarians have the opportunity to do this because to a large extent their initial decisions are largely unfettered and only second-guessed.

Bar-Hillel would argue that such value systems are clearly none of the librarian's business, and the Library Bill of Rights and various codes of ethics would at least partially agree. Certainly they would argue that one should not consciously withhold information because of its content, but if one fails to buy the item in which the information is contained, this is a qualitative decision that can be defended. That is the issue that arises when ultraconservatives and alternative press advocates complain that the library does not have their material. Librarians respond that ultraconservative literature is lacking because most of it is badly written and its arguments shoddily presented. This criticism is dangerous because it is totally subjective, but the problems with such criticism are rarely discussed in library schools.

Social Responsibility and the Librarian

Far more open are the social activists who argue that libraries cannot be neutral in the battle between right and wrong. The difficulty is, of course, in the definition of right and wrong. Sometimes this discussion takes subtle turns. The author's own writings have raised the question of whether librarians, who clearly have the obligation of helping destitute tenants find ways to avoid eviction, also have an equal obligation to help landlords look for ways to evict so that they can tear down a building and erect a shopping mall or high-priced condominium (White, 1986). A small group answers, "Of course"; a second group finds it a contrived question—always a good response for a question one does not want to answer; and a third group argues that tenants need libraries while landlords have other outlets. All three groups can be found on library school faculties and, like faculty anywhere, they do as much inculcating as teaching.

The social activists who see a proactive role for the library in helping the poor (presumably against the oppressive rich) raise issues not covered in the rather bland Bill of Rights and codes of ethics, which fight only enemies on whom all are agreed. Thus, Fay Blake (1978) has argued that libraries discriminate *de facto* against poor people because poor people do not need bibliographies. It is an intriguing argument because oppressors do not need bibliographies, either, and because understaffed librarians do not have the time to compile that many bibliographies. Michael Harris (1976) has argued for some time that the entire premise of the public library is as a capitalist contrivance to keep poor people in their place, and that Andrew Carnegie knew exactly what he was funding and why he was funding it.

It has been suggested that the public library of the future undoubtedly had the greater role of serving poor people, because the affluent would have other access to information. It is for many an attractive argument that can lead to ethical difficulties. Libraries have taken on increasing responsibility for helping the illiterate. It is in one sense a curious reversal of the classic library role, quite aside from its moral values. Libraries by their very nature serve people who know how to read, and it is the schools that have by and large failed abysmally in preparing the library's customers. If librarians now take on this responsibility, and do so without additional funding, then decisions are made that take priority and money away from other clients. How are those decisions made? It is something library schools do not teach, and perhaps it is something they cannot teach, but it is an issue to which library educators must alert and sensitize their students.

Even more curious is the issue of latchkey children. This is a social problem which on the face of it has nothing to do with libraries at all, unless the children are drawn to the library as a library rather than just as a safe, dry place. But if the reason they come is to read, then nothing stopped them before and nothing has changed.

The questions of professional ethics raised here are much broader than the simple issue of political activism urged by Henry Blanke (1989). Blanke accuses librarians of having claimed neutrality as a ploy to achieve professional status. The argument is not only dishonest because it suggests that librarians do what displeases Blanke solely as a self-serving device, but it also completely ignores the possibility that at least some librarians might opt not for neutrality but for evenhandedness as a matter of professional responsibility, even though taking political stances is obviously more emotionally rewarding.

These, then, are among the issues of professional ethics with which library schools rarely, if ever, deal. Library educators discuss how censors and bigots should be fought, but not as often about how to recognize and compensate for the librarian's personal bias. If one is pro-choice, how does that affect one's attitude toward a patron wearing a Falwell button? If one is pro-life, how does one make sure that this bias does not show? The easy (and unacceptable) answer is either that the other person is wrong (and one can substitute "bigoted" for any biases other than one's own), or that the other person has other access to information. Is this relevant?

What is the rationale for charging corporate libraries for reference access to public libraries, presumably on the basis that corporations are rich, when corporations pay taxes that support the library and are as entitled to information as anyone else? If the library wants to limit the amount of information it will provide to any client, that is another issue, but what, then, does that decision morally imply? Why do corporate librarians put up with this double standard, rather than simply say that if this is a free library to residents, then service to the resident which happens to be a corporation should also be free? Inconsistency is met with indifference instead of responsibility.

Responsibilities to Employer, Client, and Self

Different professions approach the dichotomy between the responsibilities to their professions and their responsibilities to their employers quite differently. Librarians, like social workers, find a third responsibility in a devotion to their "clients" (it has been a long time since social caseworkers have called them "cases").

Librarians nevertheless harbor considerable responsibility to their employers. They carry out some responsibilities to their clients but choose those responsibilities inconsistently. They carry little responsibility, if any, to their profession, and that, too, warrants an explanation. Librarians are extremely loyal organization men and women. As a special librarian, the author finds that example most obvious in watching his colleagues at conferences concentrating not on social involvement but on learning things to make them more effective employees. At one point in its history, the Special Libraries Association faced the possibility of a ruling from the IRS that it was not a professional association at all, but rather a business league, because its primary business and indeed its bylaws stressed improving service to the employer. This acculturation is seen clearly and immediately as former students who are now special librarians come back to lecture at library schools. They clearly represent the organization, the quality of its products, and the uniqueness of its services.

Public librarians show this organizational loyalty in a different way, most directly in their unwillingness to complain openly about inadequacies of support and in their willingness to rationalize that whatever library they are allowed to run is a good library, through a process sometimes called community analysis, which is really only a retrofitting of needs to match resources. Anyone in doubt of this should read any public library's annual report. The essence of management communication, exception reporting—the clear indication of what is not happening and not working—is not to be found. Librarians let their bosses off easily.

Responsibility to clients is unevenly carried out. While their right to access is protected, that access is limited to what is free or within the library's budget. Librarians insist that the federal government supply documents, but whether or not individuals can find what they need because of cataloging backlogs or because of a shortage of reference librarians is not seen as the same kind of moral issue. And yet, if one cannot get information, does it really matter why not? If there is a charge for interlibrary loan service or online searching, does that not impose a barrier to the use of information every bit as formidable as censorship? The response of some libraries—free or not at all—does not provide a solution if the result is not at all. The battle on behalf of library clients as a moral imperative is therefore halfhearted, or at least inconsistent. Huge cataloging backlogs or too few reference librarians are just as effective a form of censorship, particularly for those who have no alternatives. Not blowing the whistle on funding bodies makes librarians accessories in censorship.

Responsibilities for ethical conduct toward library support staff are equally haphazard. Librarians agree that staff salaries are low and that it is unfair for public library clerks to work evenings and weekends at regular pay while other city employees are routinely compensated at premium rates. There is commiseration, but that is all. However, perhaps the library profession's greatest ethical shortcoming is in the way it treats itself. It fails to protect itself by letting others into it, either because of administrative pressures by university presidents or presidents of the United States, or because of the rationalizations that unqualified staff must be used because there is no money to hire qualified staff. Doctors would never do this. In the absence of physicians, what physicians are supposed to do does not get done, and so money is found for more physicians. The result is not worse medicine, it is better medicine. The result for librarians is worse libraries, and nobody else even knows!

ONE APPROACH TO THE TEACHING OF ETHICS

The role of library education is not to provide answers to these questions, because they have no right or wrong answers, but rather to make students aware of the complexity of problems and options, and to make them understand the potential conflicts between their professional responsibilities and what they may see as their societal responsibilities. Can they differ? Certainly they can. What happens then? One might know what one would do but still have no right to instill one's value system under the pretense of teaching. Not at the graduate level, certainly. Library educators are teachers, not trainers or indoctrinators.

The author makes heavy use of case studies, his own and others, to illustrate issues in the classroom. Students almost immediately head for solutions rather than analysis, and it takes half a semester to wean the most articulate and self-assured away from solutions and toward analysis. Dilemmas involving people usually have at least two and sometimes far more alternatives and viewpoints, and ultimately one must choose, sometimes among several alternatives that are excellent, sometimes in situations in which none of the alternatives are very good. It is important that one understands the problem before one attempts a solution. Perhaps this is where Josephson's golden rule approach needs to be modified: Understand the client so that you can do unto them as they would have you do unto them. In practice, however, this causes problems, as any manager can verify.

The author's role in the classroom in attempting to awaken this analytical approach to ethical considerations is to challenge and question everything students say to make them defend it. Devil's advocate is played with their approaches to make sure that they have considered every possible idea that they emotionally reflect in their other dispassionate role as a professional. Of course, the author also has personal feelings and is considered by some to be quite opinionated. However, he understands that this does not matter because in his role as educator he prepares students to be able to deal with the ethical decisions they will have to make later.

CONCLUSION

Education for professional ethics is a preparation for life in a complex and pressure-filled world in which the pressures will be particularly to conform, to compromise, to get along, to avoid "rocking the boat." Perhaps doctors and lawyers understand these pitfalls better than library educators do; at least they spend more time talking about them. Yet newspapers are full of stories about doctors and lawyers who violate this trust. Are librarians, therefore, more trustworthy? Or is it simply that their violations of professional ethics are not considered important enough by outsiders to be noticed? It is one of the paradoxical temptations in the library field that, despite the fact that librarians have very little power and very low salaries, in this area they can get away with a great deal.

Perhaps education for the acceptance of professional ethics is really only an education in decision analysis and self-discipline. But a one-year program that teaches a long list of reference sources and *AACR2* interpretations that employers would prefer schools to teach gets in the way of this sort of education, which continues to get short shrift. The curriculum will continue to concentrate on the easy stuff—on the bookburner-bashing already in the literature—and end up congratulating librarians for their own high moral and ethical standards without instilling in them the knowledge of their own values.

Issues of professional ethics require the painful balancing of contradictory values. For example, stopping drunk driving is desirable, but if random breathalizer tests are not desirable, then how does one get from A to B? Society is full of such contradictory pressures and so, of course, are libraries. If students do not see that, it is only because they have created a very selective professional responsibility approach for themselves. Bashing the Blume and Vonnegut banners is important, but it is also easy, and librarians are inclined to do it anyway. The problems are more complex, and morality and ethics are easy to define only if everything except what is "known" to be true is ignored.

One does not have to look very far in today's society to see the complexity of moral issues. The battles between pro-choice and pro-life forces are between two groups absolutely certain of the ethical morality of their course, and that simply forecloses debate. Moral attitude finds little need to discuss. Librarians as human beings are every bit as likely to come down emotionally on one side or the other, but as librarians should serve the need for ammunition (if they bother to seek ammunition) of both groups. Words and slogans do not help here, because peace, humanism, decency, and justice are claimed as their own unique preserve by all causes. The author's own rule of thumb is that the more aggressively any faction proclaims its own saintliness, the more suspect it becomes.

Professional dilemmas for librarians come in their responsibility to things, causes, and people they do not like. That is not nearly as easy, and not nearly as much fun. But that is what professionalism means, and it is the library educator's job to at least make sure that students understand and recognize their own upcoming responsibilities — to their employers, patrons, subordinate staff members, professional colleagues, and world in which they live. Anybody who says all of this is easy and obvious is either a fool or a liar, and those are two types not needed anywhere in academia, but certainly not in professional graduate education.

REFERENCES

Blake, F. M. (1978). Let my people know: Access to information in a post industrial society. *Wilson Library Bulletin, 52*(5), 392-399.

Blanke, H. T. (1989). Librarianship & political values: Neutrality or commitment? *Library Journal, 114* (12), 39-43.

Harris, M. H. (1976). Portrait in parodox: Commitment and ambivalence in American librarianship. *Libri, 26*(4), 281-301.

Kochen, M. (1987). Ethics and information science. *Journal of the American Society for Information Science, 38*(3), 206-210.

Levitt, S. (1960). *The Andersonville trial.* New York: Random House.

Moyers, B. (1989). Ethical dilemmas. *New Age Journal, vi*(4), 42-45, 97-100.

Serebnick, J. (1981). Book reviews and the selection of potentially controversial books in public libraries. *Library Quarterly, 51*(3), 390-409.

White, H. S. (1986). Public libraries and the political process. *Library Journal, 111*(11), 49-51.

White, H. S. (1990). My truths are more moral than your biases. *Library Journal, 115*(1), 72-73.

CHARLES A. BUNGE

Professor
School of Library and Information Studies
University of Wisconsin-Madison

Ethics and the Reference Librarian

INTRODUCTION

The intent of this paper is to help reference librarians and others answer the question, "What is ethical reference practice?" or "How should the librarian act or behave in providing reference service?" The emphasis will be on the individual reference librarian's interactions with clients. Ethical concerns of the library as a whole or of librarians in general, such as fees for service and equitable availability of service, will be left to other papers at this institute. The paper will set out a group of norms or obligations that should guide the reference librarian's service to clients. Guidelines for following these norms will be put forward, along with strategies for applying them.

Issues to be discussed in the paper, examples of situations that raise ethical concerns, and ideas for dealing with them have been drawn from the literature on reference ethics, especially the issue of *The Reference Librarian* that was devoted to the topic (Katz & Fraley, 1982). Statements in the American Library Association (ALA) 1981 "Statement on Professional Ethics" (ALA, 1981, pp. 63-64) that are particularly relevant to reference librarians are discussed, as are the norms articulated in the section on "Ethics of Service" in the guidelines of the Reference and Adult Services Division (RASD) of ALA (ALA, RASD, 1979).

The conceptual framework for this paper relies heavily on Michael D. Bayles'(1981) work, *Professional Ethics.* Helpful insights on the complexities of public services practice and coping behaviors that public services professionals develop have come from Michael Lipsky's (1980) book, *Street-Level Bureaucracy,* and from Jane Robbins (1972). The emphasis in this paper on the importance of continual reflection by the reference librarian on his or her reference practice and how it can be made to conform to ethical norms has been influenced strongly by

Donald A. Schön's (1983) *The Reflective Practitioner.* All these works would be useful reading for reference librarians who wish to understand and improve their reference practice, including its ethical dimension.

THE REFERENCE LIBRARIAN'S OBLIGATIONS TO CLIENTS

The Professional-Client Relationship

The distinctiveness of the ethical concerns of reference librarians derives from the reference librarian's distinctive role in library and information services, i.e., direct service to individual clients. What ethical obligations does the reference librarian have to clients? The following section will explore this question by discussing the professional-client relationship in general and then several specific obligations that derive from that relationship.

As Bayles says, "The central issue in the professional-client relationship is the allocation of responsibility and authority for decision making—who makes what decisions" (p. 61). Obviously, models of such allocation can range from one in which the client has the most authority and responsibility, through a relationship of equality, to one in which the professional has the most authority and responsibility.

For example, many of the articles on the reference interview are based on what Bayles calls the "paternalism" model, wherein the professional is in the superior position and is making decisions on behalf of the client for his or her well-being (pp. 65-68). One reason that is given for conducting a reference interview is that the client does not really know what he or she needs. Also, some of the articles on ethics in reference service pose dilemmas based on the assumption that reference librarians need to protect inquirers from obtaining information that would be harmful to them, whether information on committing suicide or "shortcut" materials that would undermine the learning intended by a teacher (Is It . . . Do, 1983; Delaney, 1955).

This conception of the reference librarian-client relationship is a poor one on which to base ethical decisions because it fails to recognize the knowledge of their own situation that clients bring to the reference desk, it fails to recognize the competence that clients have to recognize when their information needs are met, and it denies clients the freedom to direct their own lives. Dorothy Broderick (1982) writes that value judgments derived from this paternalistic view of clients put librarians in the same category as censors.

> They, too, are sure that if the potential for misuse of information exists, it will be misused. This is a very poor view of the human race, one that I do not share. I am convinced that most people, given

> access to all points of view, will choose for themselves that which is least destructive personally and for society. I worry far more about decisions based on ignorance than those based on information, . . . (p. 22)

If the paternalistic model is not a satisfactory basis for settling ethical dilemmas, perhaps a better model is one wherein authority and responsibility are shared equally. Readers of reference literature will recognize this model as the one underlying arguments for client-centered or counseling approaches to reference service, as well as arguments for demystifying (or even deprofessionalizing) reference service. As Bayles points out, this concept of a professional-client relationship based on an agreement between equals, in which there are mutual obligations and rights (the "contract" model), "accords well with the liberal values of freedom and equality of opportunity" (p. 63).

However, for many reference transactions this model assumes an equality that does not fully pertain. Normally, the professional's knowledge and expertise in finding information exceed considerably that of the client. Also, to the extent that the information need of the client is an important one, the client has more at stake in the reference encounter than does the reference librarian, placing the client in a weaker position.

What is needed, then, is a conception of the reference librarian-client relationship that not only recognizes the professional's superior knowledge and expertise but also recognizes the importance of the client's competence, authority, and responsibility. Using a concept from the law, Bayles calls the appropriate model a "fiduciary relationship."

> In a fiduciary relationship, both parties are responsible and their judgments are given consideration. Because one party is in a more advantageous position, he or she has special obligations to the other. The weaker party depends upon the stronger in ways in which the other does not and so must *trust* the stronger party. (p. 68)

In a typical situation, the reference librarian is consulted by clients with a wide range of levels of competence and knowledge regarding the subject areas of their questions, available information sources, and strategies for using them. This means that in some (perhaps most) reference encounters, the relationship with the client will be close to a contract between equals, while in others, the librarian will need to assume relatively more responsibility for making recommendations and even decisions on the client's behalf. This variation in the reference situation is one of the main reasons that ethical prescriptions designed to cover all cases are so unhelpful to the reference librarian. The fiduciary model accommodates this variety, allowing the client as much authority and responsibility as is warranted by his or her ability to make decisions. Normally, the reference librarian will have superior technical knowledge and expertise regarding information sources and their use, and it is appropriate that the librarian make judgments in these matters. However, the librarian does not have expertise in the inquirer's values, in how the information should be used, or in the inquirer's goals in life. These are areas in which the client should be allowed the fullest possible freedom to make judgments and decisions.

The fiduciary ethical model for the reference librarian-client relationship emphasizes the obligation the librarian has to be worthy of the client's trust. A useful way to explore ethical norms for librarians in their relationships with clients is to ask what obligations the librarian must meet in order to be worthy of the client's trust that reference service will be provided "in a manner that promotes the client's interest—including the freedom to make decisions regarding his or her life" (Bayles, 1981, p. 70). The next few paragraphs will discuss the obligations of competence, diligence, confidentiality, independence of judgment, honesty, and candor.

Competence

Competence is the most crucial obligation. No matter how hard reference librarians work at other ethical mandates, if they are incompetent, they are unworthy of their clients' trust. Both the ALA and RASD ethics statements require competent ("skillful," "accurate") responses to inquiries. This obligation has two important aspects: That the reference librarian not attempt to provide information of a sort he or she is not competent to provide and that the reference librarian be as competent as possible in providing the information that he or she and the employing agency purport to be able to provide.

The obligation not to practice in areas where one is not competent is the basis for the proscription against the reference librarian's providing medical or legal advice. Because the lengthy training periods required for doctors and lawyers are well known, the librarian's lack of competence to provide advice in these areas is quite obvious. However, the literature contains other examples, such as the provision of the librarian's evaluative opinions on consumer products and recommending particular service providers (Wood & Renford, 1982; Schanck, 1979; Is It . . . Mechanic, 1983).

There are various guidelines that might be used to assist the reference librarian in acting ethically in this regard. One such guideline is to avoid providing information personally that cannot be documented or confirmed in information sources, except in limited circumstances where the reference librarian's special knowledge or training gives him or her competence to provide substantive information of the sort required. This was the tenor of most of the responses to the ALA Ethics

Committee's question regarding the ethics of a librarian's recommending an auto mechanic to a patron (Is It . . . Mechanic, 1983). Another guideline is to try always to make a distinction between assisting the inquirer in finding information sources or using them to locate desired information, and interpreting the meaning of the information found or advising on a course of action based on the information found. The librarian has special knowledge and expertise (i.e., competence) in the former but not in the latter. Of course, this is simpler to say than to do in many instances because the line between explaining how to use a tool and interpreting what an entry in a tool means is often a fine one. Peter C. Schanck (1979) has some useful advice on how to avoid crossing this line (pp. 63-64).

A key factor in this matter is the client's perception of the situation. It is important that the reference librarian be honest and candid with the patron regarding the complexity of the information sought and its interpretation, the limitations on the information that is available, and the kind of assistance the reference librarian is providing. Schanck recommends avoiding giving the patron the impression that "This is the law" and advises attempting to get the patron to understand the complexity of the law (p. 63). Other authors offer similar advice for health-related information (Wood & Renford, pp. 78-79). In areas such as law and health, it is important that reference clients understand that, while the library attempts to obtain the most complete and current information feasible, there may well be more recent and more complete information and that consulting a competent health or legal professional may be advisable. It is also important that the reference librarian try to have the client understand the nature of the assistance that is being provided, i.e., assistance in finding and using information rather than in interpreting the information or deciding on a course of action based on it.

The other aspect of the obligation of competence, i.e., that the librarian be as competent as possible in assisting clients in obtaining and using the information they need, is an especially troublesome area. Every reference librarian is all too aware that the more one knows about information sources, whether in print or electronic formats, the more one has yet to learn. The same can be said of the librarian's knowledge and skill in the varying information needs of his or her clients and the complexities of interacting with them effectively.

Two obvious guidelines here are that the reference librarian continue learning and that colleagues with specialized knowledge be involved on questions that go beyond his or her competence. In practice, these guidelines can raise more dilemmas than they settle. As Samuel Rothstein (1982) points out, most reference librarians receive inadequate institutional support for pursuing continuing education (p. 4). The schedules of reference librarians often preclude getting assistance from a colleague except on a considerably delayed basis. However, at the least, the obligation of competence requires that reference librarians, individually and in staffing groups, reflect on the limits of their competence, pursue all feasible opportunities for maintaining and improving knowledge and skills, and attempt to make the best match possible between the needs of individual clients and the competencies of the staff members who assist them.

Honesty and candor with the client regarding the reference librarian's competence are important here as well. Potential disadvantage or even harm to the client due to assistance from a reference librarian who is not fully knowledgeable or skilled in the area of the client's question can be considerably lessened if the reference librarian explains the limitations on the assistance that he or she is able to provide, outlines alternatives (e.g., consulting a specialist colleague, referral to another source), and allows the client freedom of decision in the matter.

Diligence

Another obligation following from the requirement that the reference librarian be worthy of the client's trust is that the professional exercise sufficient care and effort in responding to inquiries. A very high level of competence will be for naught if the reference librarian does not apply it to reference questions with diligence. Rothstein notes that "It has been pointed out that reference librarians are frequently less than assiduous in the information service they render . . . ," citing failure to conduct adequate reference interviews and the findings of various reference evaluation studies as evidence (pp. 4-5).

Why should such seemingly unethical behavior by reference librarians be so prevalent? A great many such lapses from diligence result from habits and patterns of behavior borne of what Rothstein calls the "extraordinarily difficult circumstances" under which reference questions are answered.

> The reference librarians must serve anonymous clients whose needs and capabilities they cannot really know; they must be prepared to give instant answers to questions covering almost every conceivable subject; they must operate in full public view and under harassing requirements of speed. (p. 5)

Reference librarians develop coping mechanisms to deal with such circumstances, including truncated reference interviews, hurried use of information sources, and rationing time among users—sometimes treating different types of users or questions differently.

Such coping behavior can represent a necessary balancing of obligations to various clients and can result in fuller and more equitable service to more people than would otherwise be the case. Unfortunately, without reflection and monitoring, this behavior can feed on itself and develop into habits of poor reference practice and discrimination among clients or questions on indefensible grounds.

How does the reference librarian work through the ethical dilemmas involved in the obligation to provide diligent service under difficult circumstances? Surely, an important step is to identify the characteristics and behaviors associated with effective reference service, to make such service the standard against which one compares one's practice, and to attempt to make such behaviors habitual. Seeking support and evaluation from reference colleagues can be helpful in this regard. When conflicting demands and time pressures seem to mandate providing less than ideal service, it can be helpful to concentrate on the client at hand (i.e., to honor to the fullest extent possible one's obligation of diligence to that client) and to try not to overcompromise, so as to provide poor service to many clients rather than at least adequate service to a reasonable number. Finally, if the situation seems to demand discrimination among types of patrons or questions in the allocation of time and effort (rather than using the principle of first come-first served), the reference librarian should make judgments based on principles of equality of access (e.g., offering more help to the näive or confused user than to the self-assured) or on the distinctive role and primary clientele of the library rather than on personal biases or preferences.

Confidentiality

Privacy is a central value in American society. Its crucial relationship to the free pursuit and use of information is recognized in both the ALA and RASD statements. Both statements require that reference librarians not reveal information about their clients, either about the information they seek or use, or information about the client gained from the reference interaction. Most dilemmas in this area of ethics involve the possibility of inadvertently revealing information that should be confidential and deciding when revealing confidential information might be permissible because it is in the client's best interest or in the best interest of society at large.

The potential for violating the client's privacy is the reason for the injunction that reference librarians not discuss with others their inter-actions with patrons, whether as interesting staff room conversation or with persons outside the library. Potential for betraying confidential information also arises from library recordkeeping systems, including those for interlibrary loan or online search services. M. Kathleen Cook and Mary K. Isbell (1986) have useful suggestions in this regard, including limiting access to such records, limiting the length of time the records are kept, limiting client identification on the records, and revealing information only with client approval.

The question of when information about a client and his or her use of library resources might ethically be revealed is a complex one. Surely, at times, service to the client would be improved if the question were discussed with a colleague. A useful guideline here is to seek the client's permission for such discussion. When this is not feasible, perhaps the best guide is the reference librarian's good faith assessment of what the client would approve, having assessed the necessity for sharing confidential information and the colleague's commitment to confidentiality.

In some circumstances the reference librarian becomes aware that two clients could benefit if each knew that the other was working on a particular problem. The work of each client or of the company that operates the information service could possibly be enhanced if one client knew of the other's work. Here again, obtaining the client's permission to discuss his or her information use with others is an obvious guideline.

Sometimes, the needs of other members of society or of society at large seem to suggest revealing information about a client's use of information. Mark Stover (1987) uses examples of clients who use the information for known or suspected criminal activity and of helping a teacher determine whether a student library user has committed plagiarism. A more general discussion of obligations to such third parties is the subject of another section of this paper. It is sufficient here to articulate the guideline of revealing confidential information only after very careful consideration, only when there is a high degree of certainty that serious negative consequences will result from maintaining confidence, or when required by competent legal authority.

Independence of Judgment
Both the ALA and RASD ethics statements specify that the service provided by the librarian should not be influenced by personal philosophies and attitudes and should not be compromised by conflicting financial interests of the librarian. If the reference librarian does not apply his or her special knowledge and skills to make judgments that will promote the client's best interests, the librarian is not worthy of the client's trust.

Judith Farley (1982) mentions the potential for unethical reference behavior that arises with requests for information on topics on which the reference librarian has a strongly held philosophical position, and Broderick (1982) discusses various biases of reference librarians that can influence reference practice. Obviously, a reference librarian who allows such personal philosophies and attitudes to influence the amount and quality of reference that is provided is unworthy of the client's trust and is acting unethically.

This is not to say that the reference librarian should be without personal beliefs and attitudes. In fact, the more fully aware the librarian is of his or her beliefs and attitudes, the more likely he or she is to be able to keep them from detrimentally influencing professional practice. The best approach is continual awareness and reflection so as to keep one's judgments from being clouded or colored by personal philosophies and biases.

Broderick points out that a written reference service policy can also help in reducing the influence of personal biases on reference practice (p. 19). If a library or its reference staff believes that restrictions are necessary in responding to certain types of questions or certain client groups in order to allocate resources and to serve the primary clientele appropriately, such policies should be arrived at carefully and should be made known to the public so that users and potential users can make choices and decisions with full information. Point 6.4 of the RASD statement makes this point along with the point that such rules and practices should be carried out impartially.

Financial conflicts of interest are another source of loss of independence of judgment. John C. Swan (1982) points out that one's judgments and information provision regarding information sources can be influenced by special relationships that one has with a particular tool or publisher, e.g., as a salesperson, consultant, or reviewer. Steps that Swan recommends to minimize such conflicts include making clear to the client one's special relation with reference resources, refraining absolutely from allowing outside work to creep into regular reference work, and "careful, honest scrutiny of oneself . . ." in each reference situation (p. 109-110).

The growth of fee-based information services has been accompanied by an increased potential for conflicts of interest for the reference librarian. The freelance, for-fee reference librarian is involved in a conflict between obligations to the client and the need to make a living that cannot be entirely removed. Bayles writes that such conflicts are inherent in private practice professions. He points out that they can be minimized through firm agreements with clients as to what will be done and its total cost. Where the cost cannot reasonably be estimated in advance, the professional should try to develop alternative fee systems (e.g., standard fees for certain categories of service) that will reduce the potential for financial issues interfering with independent professional judgments regarding what will best serve the client's interests (p. 78).

When the reference librarian is employed both at a "free" reference
desk and by a fee-based information service (whether within the same
library or outside), obvious potential conflicts of interest arise. Here
again, it is easier to write into ethics codes an injunction not to let such
considerations cloud judgments than it is to tread the line between
referrals to fee-based services that are truly in the client's best interest
and decisions to refer that are based on the librarian's (perhaps uncon-
scious) desire to keep the fee-based service's volume at a viable level.
Sometimes, honest reflection will cause the reference librarian to conclude that avoiding unethical conflict of interest would be so difficult
as to preclude holding both positions. In other situations, honesty and
candor with clients along with continuous monitoring of one's judgments
and behavior will result in ethical practice. Swan's advice, cited above,
of honest scrutiny of oneself in each situation holds here as well.

Honesty and Candor
The importance of dealing with the reference client honestly and
candidly has been mentioned a number of times above, so that only a
summary treatment is needed here. As Bayles says, "By definition, a
dishonest professional is not worthy of a client's trust" (p. 71). The
ethical obligation not to lie to a client is clear and is probably seldom
violated by reference librarians.

The obligation for candor is not so straightforward, though it is at
the heart of the fiduciary relationship with one's clients. In this relationship, the reference librarian respects the judgment of the client and
involves the client in decisions regarding the search for information. If
the reference librarian withholds or manipulates information that would
help the client participate fully in such decisions, the librarian is acting
on his or her own judgments of what is good for the client, and the
relationship is paternalistic.

Because candor involves the amount and kind of information to be
shared with the client rather than simply its truth or falsity, meeting
this obligation involves the reference librarian's continually making
judgments regarding how much and what kinds of information regarding
the situation and options that are open to the client should be shared
with him or her. Examples of areas where the issue of candor arises
that have been used elsewhere in this paper include sharing knowledge
regarding the reference librarian's competence and the reference collection's completeness regarding a particular question, informing the
client regarding options available such as taking the question to another
source of information, and disclosing the reference librarian's financial
interests that might cause conflicts of interest. Certainly, candor re-

garding fees for service and options available to the client in attempting to gain the best value for fees paid is very important.

Are there situations where full candor is not desirable or necessary? The most obvious one would be when candor with one client would violate confidentiality with another. Another is when honest reflection convinces the reference librarian that sharing of information would not affect the client's decisions and would only result in unnecessarily taking the time of the client and the librarian. The best overall guideline is for the reference librarian to ask in each situation, "How can I best help my client make judgments and decisions regarding the pursuit and use of information that will be in his or her best interest?"

OBLIGATIONS TO THIRD PARTIES

The ethical dilemmas that receive the most attention in the literature of reference ethics concern conflicts between the reference librarian's obligations to a client and obligations to others, including society at large. Perhaps the best-known example is Robert Hauptman's (1976) experiment, wherein he asked reference librarians for information on constructing a small bomb that would blow up a home (pp. 626-627). Other examples include requests for information from city directories that could result in invasion of the privacy of those listed, requests for information that might result in or facilitate illegal activities, and requests that the reference librarian commit dishonest or illegal acts in the pursuit of information (Prokop & McClure, 1982; O'Brien, 1982).

Such conflicts raise some of the most difficult problems of professional ethics. Because librarianship has a special role and function in society and because the professional-client relationship is crucial to that function, the reference librarian must give special attention to clients that is not given to others. Thus, such obligations as diligence in serving the client's needs, confidentiality, and use of judgment independent of influence by social or political considerations are of primary importance.

On the other hand, the special function of librarianship and its authority to devise and follow special ethical obligations are for the good of society as a whole. That is, reference librarians, by carrying out their obligations to their clients, enhance the functioning of a democratic society without which the client would not be able to use the information provided. It does not make sense, then, that professional ethics would require actions that would be contrary to the values of a democratic society or that would undermine its operation or viability. When conflicts arise between the reference librarian's obligations to clients and to others, the issue is whether or not the special obligations to the client should be limited by general obligations to others and to the values of a democratic society.

Hauptman (1976) frames the issue incorrectly when he describes the dilemma as a conflict between professional ethics and personal ethics and accuses reference librarians who provided "bomb" information of failure to make personal ethical judgments and of simplistically or unthinkingly following professional ethics. Surely, purely personal ethical norms, such as those based on religious or political beliefs that are not part of the laws and values of a democratic society, cannot restrict professional obligations in the librarian's practice. Conflicts between obligations to the reference client and personal religious beliefs (e.g., aversion to certain religious practices or birth control methods) must be resolved in favor of the obligation to assist the client diligently and with independence of judgment. On the other hand, in order to assure ethical behavior, the reference librarian must make a personal commitment to the norms of professional ethics and to the values of a democratic society to which professional norms must bear a functional relationship. Thus, the conflict is not between professional ethics and personal ethics but is between special obligations to clients and general obligations to third parties within society as a whole. Acting ethically in particular instances is a matter of weighing responsibilities so as to produce a balance that most fully enhances the values of a democratic society.

Bayles (1981) further points out that the problem of conflicts between obligations to clients and to third parties is especially acute for employee professionals (as opposed to those in private practice) because such professionals can be caught between the demands of the employer and what they consider best for the client (p. 23). Reference librarians sometimes experience such conflicts between policies and practices of the library and what would best serve the needs of an individual client. An additional concern is the fact that the library in which the reference librarian works has been set up and is funded to serve the functions of a parent institution or organization (e.g., an educational institution or a corporation), adding other possible areas of conflict between obligations to the client and to others. Robert M. Pierson (1967), for example, says that reference librarians in libraries committed to the support of education should take this into account when students ask for help in shortcutting school assignments.

What general obligations to others might limit the reference librarian's obligations to the client? Because governance by law and truthfulness (if not full candor) are basic values in a democratic society, the professional should not act illegally or dishonestly even if the client's access to information would seem to be enhanced thereby. Compliance with copyright laws and honoring agreements with vendors of information sources are examples of areas where the potential for acting illegally on behalf of clients is said to be especially high. The same general obligation or principle would make it unethical to assist a patron to commit an illegal act or one that is immoral according to the values of society.

The obligation of honesty and for honoring agreements into which one has entered might also underlie the reference librarian's obligations to the employing library and to the larger institution that the library serves. To the extent that the reference librarian has made an explicit or implied agreement to carry out the policies of the library, or to the extent that the library's existence and support is understood to derive from its agreement to serve the objectives of a parent institution (e.g., the educational goals of an educational institution), obligations to the policies and functions of the library and its parent institution might restrict the librarian's obligations to assist the client in obtaining the information he or she requests.

Another fundamental value of a democratic society is the protection of people from injury by others. This means that the reference librarian's obligation to clients to act with diligence and confidentiality in assisting them to find and use the information they request is limited by the obligation that such actions not result in injury to third persons. Hauptman (1988) argues that this is the limitation that the reference librarians in his experiment should have applied (pp. 42-46).

Stating these areas of possible restrictions on the reference librarian's obligations to the client provides little help in the question-by-question attempt to balance special obligations to the client and general obligations to others. What guidelines might the reference librarian follow in attempting to weigh and balance these obligations and to act ethically? It is useful to reflect on the fiduciary model of the professional-client relationship. This model considers clients to be competent, responsible persons. As Swan puts it, we "put our faith in the connection between knowledge and responsible action" (Wiener, 1987, p. 162). An important guideline, then, is to consider the probability (or the reference librarian's certainty) that violation of the values of society or injury to third parties will actually occur. Swan points out that "Reading about bomb building is not the same as bombing; reading about suicide is not the same as committing it . . . (p. 162). Surely, merely the potential that the infor-mation might be used for illegal purposes or to injure someone, or even the vague suspicion that this will be the case, is not sufficient reason to limit one's obligation to one's client to assist in finding requested information. However, faced with reasonably clear and certain knowl-edge that the client intends to use the requested information for illegal or injurious purposes, the reference librarian could ethically refuse to provide requested assistance.

Another guideline is to consider the seriousness of the potential harm to third parties. Reference librarians argue, for example, that the invasion of privacy and harassment incurred by persons whose names and addresses are obtained from directories in the library are not serious enough to balance limiting their obligation to provide access to information in published sources. Faced with the use of information for clearly illegal purposes or for violence toward other persons, the same librarians would strike a different balance.

Another useful way to look at this balance is to consider the result that might come from limiting the librarian's obligations to the client. For example, students who cannot rely on the confidentiality of their interactions with reference librarians (as would be the case should the librarian report to teachers suspected plagiarism or "shortcuts" on assignments) are likely to avoid using the reference librarian's service and perhaps libraries generally. The detrimental effects that this could have on the students' well-being would more than offset obligations to society or to the educational objectives of the library and the school it serves.

As an overall aid to finding the proper balance among obligations, Bayles proposes that the professional ask what balance a reasonable person with liberal values would conclude best promotes the values of a democratic society. In this process one asks whether one would rather live in a society where the balance is struck in favor of one obligation or another (pp. 99-100). Surely, such a person would conclude that he or she would not want to live in a society where access to information and privacy in its use are restricted because the information *might* be put to a use that is harmful to the user or to others. On the other hand, a reasonable person would recognize that governance by law is fundamental to a democratic society and would not want to live in a society where reference librarians were obligated to use any means, legal or not, to serve their clients' needs, or where professional norms required librarians knowingly to assist clients in the performance of acts of violence toward others.

Bayles and Hauptman, following Kant's categorical imperative, suggest that ethical decisions be tested as to whether or not the actions that would follow from them can be universalized, i.e., whether the same action would be taken in a later similar case (Bayles, 1981, p. 100; Hauptman, 1988, p. 2). Such consideration can keep the reference librarian's judgments from being unduly influenced by unique aspects of the present situation and can remind the librarian to seek basic principles to guide individual decisions and actions.

Finally, the reference librarian should always keep in mind Hauptman's advice to follow Kant's dictum that we "always treat human beings as ends and never merely as means. In other words, always consider the dignity and human worth of each individual" (Hauptman, 1988, p. 2). Such consideration will help give the librarian's special obligations to the client proper weight in balancing apparently conflicting ethical demands. Even if the librarian decides that special obligations to the client must be limited by obligations to others or to society, the client should be treated with the honesty, courtesy, and respect that will affirm his or her worth as a human individual.

CONCLUSION

This paper has attempted to provide a philosophical or conceptual framework for considering the ethical concerns of the reference librarian. It has argued that central to the professional-client relationship is the trust in the reference librarian that the client must have. In order to be worthy of this trust, the reference librarian is obligated to act with competence, diligence, confidentiality, independence of judgment, honesty, and candor.

The paper has also tried to show that the obligations of the reference librarian to the client bear a functional relationship to the values of a democratic society and to obligations to third parties that derive from these values. Some of the most complex ethical dilemmas of reference librarians arise from the need to balance special obligations to clients and ordinary obligations to others and to society as a whole.

The paper has provided guidelines and principles that can be used to address ethical issues and dilemmas that arise in reference work, along with strategies for applying the guidelines in particular situations. Central to applying these strategies is the realization that reference service is a very complex undertaking and that it is often practiced under very difficult circumstances of limited resources and almost unlimited expectations. The development of coping behaviors to make the reference situation more manageable and less stressful is a very human response; but without monitoring, these behaviors can become habits of response to clients and their information needs that do not serve librarians' ethical obligations to their clients or to the values of society such as governance by law, freedom, equality of opportunity, prevention of harm, welfare, and privacy.

In order to act ethically in reference practice, the reference librarian must continually be in a reflective dialogue with the situation as it unfolds. As each encounter with a client develops and the librarian becomes familiar with the client's information need, the reference librarian must ask, "How should I act so as to be worthy of the trust of this client and to support and enhance the values of our democratic society?" The answer will not always be obvious or easy to implement. But if the question is not asked and the answer is not confronted, the chances of the reference librarian's acting ethically will be smaller than they should be.

REFERENCES

American Library Association. (1981). The ALA's statement on professional ethics. In Jonathan A. Lindsey and Ann E. Prentice (Eds.), *Professional ethics and librarians* (pp. 63-64). Phoenix, AZ: Oryx.

American Library Association, Reference and Adult Services Division, Standards Committee. (1979). A commitment to information services: Developmental guidelines. *RQ, 18*(3), 275-278.

Bayles, M. D. (1981). *Professional ethics*. Belmont, CA: Wadsworth.

Broderick, D. (1982). Value laden barriers to information dissemination. *Reference Librarian, 4(Summer)*, 19-23.

Cook, K. M., & Isbell, M. K. (1986). Confidentiality of online bibliographic searches: Attitudes and practices. *RQ, 25*(4), 483-487.

Delaney, J. J. (1955). Questions to hedge. *Library Journal, 80*(1), 48-50.

Farley, J. (1982). Reference ethics: A true confession. *Reference Librarian, 4(Summer)*, 13-17.

Hauptman, R. (1976). Professionalism or culpability? An experiment in ethics. *Wilson Library Bulletin, 50*(April), 626-627.

Hauptman, R. (1988). *Ethical challenges in librarianship*. Phoenix, AZ: Oryx.

Is it ethical for a librarian to recommend a mechanic? (1983). *American Libraries, 14*(May), 270.

Is it ethical to help a student find a how-to-commit-suicide manual and is that all you do? (1983). *American Libraries, 4*(November), 643.

Katz, B., & Fraley, R. A. (Eds.). (1982). Ethics and reference service. (Issue theme). *Reference Librarian, 4(Summer)*.

Lipsky, M. (1980). *Street level bureaucracy: Dilemmas of the individual in public service*. New York: Russell Sage Foundation.

O'Brien, P. M. (1982). Some ethical problems of reference service. *Reference Librarian, 4*(Summer), 123-127.

Pierson, P. M. (1967). Is Moby Dick the whale or the captain? *RQ, 7*(1), 21-24.

Prokop, M., & McClure, C. R. (1982). The public librarian and service ethics: A dilemma. *Public Library Quarterly, 3*(4), 69-82.

Robbins, J. (1972). The reference librarian: A street-level bureaucrat? *Library Journal, 97*(8), 1389-1392.

Rothstein, S. (1982). Where does it hurt? Identifying the real concerns in the ethics of reference service. *Reference Librarian, 4*(Summer), 1-12.

Schanck, P. C. (1979). Unauthorized practice of law and the legal librarian. *Law Library Journal, 72*(Winter), 57-64.

Schön, D. A. (1983). *The reflective practitioner: How professionals think in action*. New York: Basic Books.

Stover, M. (1987). Confidentiality and privacy in reference service. *RQ, 27*(Winter), 240-244.

Swan, J. C. (1982). Ethics at the reference desk: Comfortable theories and tricky practices. *Reference Librarian, 4*(Summer), 99-116.

Wiener, P. B. (1987). Mad bombers and ethical librarians: A dialog with Robert Hauptman and John Swan. *Catholic Library World, 58*(4), 161-163.
Wood, S. M., & Renford, B. L. (1982). Ethical aspects of medical reference. *Reference Librarian, 4*(Summer), 75-87.

MICHAEL B. WESSELLS

Community Library Coordinator
Timberland Regional Library
Raymond, Washington

Feeding the Hand That Bites You

INTRODUCTION

"Do to others as you would like done to you." Service providers are trained in this ethic and none more so than librarians, who live to serve the needs of others in a notoriously self-effacing manner. It is no surprise—though something of an outrage—to see "librarian" serve as a recognizable link in the chain of wimpish occupations in a political cartoon last year. With one notable exception, to be discussed later, librarians are not seen as aggressive combatants beset by enemies in a world of tooth and claw. In fact, it is hard to imagine a group less likely to have enemies than librarians.

There are questions, however, that tend to place librarians in potentially confrontational stances with other groups. For example, who will fund the library and at what level? The answer may set public librarians against local government officials, and academic and school librarians against administrators. What books should be on the shelves, who should have access to them, and in what priority? Over these questions, school and public librarians can find themselves in a face-off with irate parents and community members; academic librarians can tussle with faculty. Beneath the librarian's placid and benign exterior lie many avenues for inner pugnacity to emerge. That it does not do so more often is the result of a fortunate conjunction between an ethical imperative and practical common sense.

Practically, it is a waste of energy and poor strategy to engage in warfare before seeking a peaceful and mutually beneficial solution. Ethically, the librarian's code requires that he or she provide "the highest level of personal integrity and competence" (ALA, 1987, p. 244). The prevailing Judeo-Christian atmosphere in Western civilization implores one to love one's enemies—if not to convert them to friends, then to heap coals of fire upon their heads.

Before taking up cudgels and rushing to the barricades, librarians need to look upon enemies the way they look upon patrons and do what they do best: ascertain the patron's needs despite what may be a hazy representation of those needs, and then meet the needs in the way that makes the patron happiest without compromising one's own integrity. When conflict seems imminent, librarians should be the first to leave the trenches and explore a peaceable solution.

Steps in Conflict Resolution

There are four basic steps in this process. First, librarians must learn the language of their enemies. What are their outlooks, priorities, and goals; what do they mean by the words they use to describe situations? Librarians must grasp enough of their world-view to communicate, to provide "skillful, accurate, unbiased, and courteous responses" to any perceived or underlying "request for assistance" (p. 244).

Second, librarians must find some common ground, however tiny. The tension only rises if the focus is on issues that divide. Instead, librarians need to begin from a sense of community and establish even the smallest sense of shared purpose to create some basic credibility. They must discipline themselves that their mission is to solve a problem, not to wage a war.

Third, librarians must initially meet some need that they perceive their "enemy" to have. This establishes a context of helping, a positive momentum that keeps the focus on resolution and surprises the enemy. By not playing by the rules of war, librarians can insist upon a different relationship altogether.

Fourth, librarians can move from common ground toward their own particular needs and concerns. In this process, they can evolve from enemies to symbiotic partners and become, if not allies, at least respectful neutrals. Only if this procedure fails should a fight be initiated. By reducing the enemy's numbers, fighting energy is saved for the truly unavoidable conflicts. If this process sounds very familiar, that may be because it is basically a dressed-up description of the reference interview!

CASE STUDY 1: THE LIBRARIAN VS. CITY HALL

Two case studies will serve as examples of how it works. The first scenario deals with the public library in a small-to-medium sized town at budget time. The enemy is obvious. Not only has the city comptroller never been in the library in his life (the librarian suspects he may be a borderline illiterate), but he is not aware of the self-evident value of the library and the consequent sanctity of each budget request item.

When the final budget emerges from the smoke-filled room, there is much weeping, wailing, and gnashing of teeth. The muted complaints of the librarian are ignored or quietly filed in the drawer marked "Things to deal with after the turn of the century." Everybody knows librarians have very little political clout. That is why they have so few enemies. "Maybe we'll find some funds for the library next year." In these terms, the fight is hopeless. The library has no chance. The fault, however, is at least partly with the librarian. The city fathers are treated as enemies when in fact they should be treated as patrons. It requires a shift of mind from looking at the keeper of purse strings as an impediment to seeing that person as a patron in need of some kind of information, a need librarians are ethically bound to satisfy.

The need may be basic and simple, even rudimentary. Some years ago, the author was on a consulting expedition during which town meetings were held in several communities where library staff, community leaders, and patrons were invited to sit together and talk about the future of library service in the area. In the midst of the meeting, the angry librarian rounded on the city comptroller, demanding to know why the library budget had not been increased in several years. The city official icily retorted that she had received no request from the library, no specific itemization of need, no timely information on which to base a budget allocation. Soon, the two of them had their heads together discussing what information would be necessary for the following year's budget and how it could appropriately be presented. They had found the common ground and were fast on the road to becoming allies. It was amazing that these two key individuals had offices directly across the street from one another and had never sat down face to face to discuss how they could facilitate one another's job. The chance meeting proved very beneficial to the librarian. How much more useful would purposeful approaches to city officials on a regular basis have been, providing in advance and neatly tabulated the data that was needed. Then the brief public confrontation would not have been necessary.

Libraries are useful to their funding bodies not only in ways that are eventually self-serving, but also in other instances that city officials might never consider if left entirely to their own devices. Librarians should aggressively seek out opportunities to serve them. The author's fantasy library school has a course called The Vagaries of Local Governments 101. It deals with the madness of public library funding and the ways librarians can overcome the system through personal communication and the provision of key information at the optimum time; in other words, being the professional partners in government that they can and should be. It involves aggressively seeking out the information needs in the camp of the enemy and meeting those needs. Most cities have one or several informal communication centers. In the author's town, it is Bob Ryan's Raymond Café where one can sit down, have a cup of coffee with the mayor, and find out what is happening, interjecting at the opportune moment, "I've got that data at the library, I'll send it over this afternoon," "We can host that meeting at the library," and so on. Librarians should be as evangelical about feeding their funders as they are about literacy programs and proactive efforts aimed at other reluctant users. This is the library version of the Biblical injunction to "go out to the highways and byways and compel them to come in."

CASE STUDY 2: THE LIBRARIAN VS. THE FUNDAMENTALIST

This manner of operation comes to seem commonplace by the time one becomes a library director, and the language and outlook of funding bodies may not be so very different from those of the director. There are wider chasms to cross as one moves to the far bloodier battlefield of intellectual freedom. Here the librarian reigns proudly as the doughty warrior standing valiantly in the gap against the censor. This is the notable exception to the librarian's wimpish image, the one area where he or she is transformed from Clark Kent to his alter ego. But it is no denigration of the vital importance of these battles for intellectual freedom to suggest that a number of them need not be fought at all. For example: A mother enters the library with her child. She is home-schooling the child because she believes that secular humanism has rendered the public schools unsafe for Christian children. The child is not allowed to read fiction because it is not true, and certainly not fairy tales or myths, which the mother thinks may be demonic. Mother is a member of Citizens Against Rampant Pornography (CARP), and even attends some of their meetings, though she lets the more vocal leaders do most of the talking. The occasion of her visit to the library is her concern about a picture book with illustrations that are more explicit than she feels is right for children. She shows examples. It is her forthright contention that the book should not be on the shelves. Furthermore, she would like to see more good Christian books, especially some that argue the case against evolution.

This is a familiar scenario. Most public and school libraries have been there, and all see the signal to draw swords and defend the bastion of intellectual freedom. But the first enemy is a stereotype. Librarians can be justly proud of their role in combatting any number of sexist and racist stereotypes, but the dominant one of our time—the "Fundamentalist"—continues to be perpetuated: a closed-minded obscurantist with a narrow view of life, determined to shackle everyone else to his or her priorities because he or she is too fanatical to rise above them. There is just as much generalizable truth in this picture as there are in abhorrent racist and sexist stereotypes.

The fact is, fundamentalists are just as complex and variegated as librarians or any other group of human beings on the planet (Marsden, 1980). There is, however, a need to learn their language and the difference in how the same words are meant by nonfundamentalists. While it would take a full-length book to deal exhaustively with this topic, there are three major tendencies of thought that may characterize the fundamentalist community and which must be understood in order to bring about a meeting of the minds. At the obvious risk of generalizing and oversimplifying, the following concepts describe them in sufficient detail to see how language learning can work.

Basic Concepts of Fundamentalism

The first concept that applies to fundamentalist thought is an intense reification. Constructs that are often used metaphorically to deal with concepts and ideas are taken as quite real in fundamentalism. For instance, the devil, which is used as a symbol of ultimate evil or even as a buffoon in story and discussion, is an actual person to fundamentalists, with a real agenda and real targets. As another example, stories that are powerfully symbolic representations of inner realities are seen as reconstructions of actual historical events. This tendency to reify is at the heart of such concerns as the literal truth of the Bible, avoidance of Halloween, the Easter Bunny, and Santa Claus, and distrust of fairy tales, myths, and speculative fiction.

The second concept is a strong concentration on individualism as opposed to corporatism in religion. This manifests itself in the focus on individual salvation and person-to-person interactions, a concern with one's personal responsibility for both self and neighbor, as distinct from more general and abstract social commitments. As a rule, fundamentalists feel a personal calling to give freely and often to the last resort, whatever their own economic circumstances, where in other Christian traditions there is more a focus on corporate action. How else could people like Jim Bakker bilk so many individuals out of so much money? Yet, when this example is used to characterize the fundamentalists, attention is on the crook rather than on the thousands of generous people who put their money where his mouth was.

The third concept of note is a cosmic dualism—an ongoing battle between good and evil that is of universal importance and in which the battleground is not only the individual but all places and concepts with which the individual comes in contact. In terms of this conflict, there is a perceived cause for alarm in the fragile nature of our society constantly under bombardment from evil and ever in danger of immediate disaster.

The ultimate future of any individual depends completely upon action being taken within a timeframe of extreme urgency. Most nonfundamentalists seem to live within a world view encompassing the stable continuation of the universe more or less infinitely for all practical purposes. Those people particularly alert to environmental and nuclear issues may feel an inner dread for the world of their children and grandchildren, or even for the next decade. For the fundamentalist, however, there not only is no assurance that the universe will continue indefinitely, but a positive guarantee that it will not, that a catastrophic end is in the plan. There is a continual haunting fear that this event is already on the calendar for next week. When this occurs, the sheep will be separated from the goats forever. In this context, then, efforts to bring people over to the "right" side must be made now because tomorrow may be too late. It may be salutary to remind oneself that the constant harassment of the "unsaved," which one may view as intrusive and wrongheaded, is rooted in a genuine and generous concern for the ultimate welfare of total strangers.

The combination of these three ingredients—reification, individual responsibility, and cosmic dualism—provides the driving force behind much of what is quickly and rightly labelled censorship. The chain of logic can then be followed from the unprovable but also irrefutable cosmic dualism through the responsibility of the individual for not only him- or herself and his or her family, but for other people as well. If the concepts by which one explains and understands this situation are seen as concrete and present in a literal way, what other way should one reasonably and ethically act but the very way fundamentalists are observed to act?

Finding a Common Ground

There are, of course, negative factors in the equation that are already very familiar. The sense of individual responsibility may be distorted into a tendency to judge and control others. Obsessive concern with the important cosmic battle may induce a fear reaction that blocks open acceptance of new and different ideas. (Would that librarians were free of similar tendencies!) But there is a strong common ground between the fundamentalist, would-be censor and the librarian. That common ground is the ineradicable belief that the book is important—that what people read or view has a very real and vital impact on their lives, and that libraries matter.

When librarians face the hypothetical, censorious mother described previously, they start from this common ground. The first thing to do is meet a need. Librarians, being natural psychologists, know that people first of all want to be heard and understood, but it is not so obvious that people also need to be taken seriously, as if their point of view is at least arguable, defensible, and deserving of more than derision. This was the point of learning their language.

The first step, then, is to listen with an empathetic ear—to make it clear to this mother that her problem is a serious one and that it is apparent how, given her premises and understanding, the problem needs a solution that is satisfactory for all. Reflective techniques and other emotionally neutral interactive skills used so proficiently in reference interviews should be employed here. Immediately, the librarian and patron are on strong common ground; the librarian can pounce upon this aspect of her present problem to meet a need right at the outset. Instead of a knee-jerk negative to the censorship request, the librarian can begin with a focus on collection building: "More Christian books? The anti-evolution viewpoint? An excellent suggestion. Are there titles or authors you might recommend?" Thus can be satisfied both the patron's need and the librarian's ethical imperative to reflect differing points of view in a balanced collection. This particular case is aided by the growing number of readable Christian books that meet any reasonable criteria for selection. Even borderline materials that are not particularly cogent or well-written can be added if they meet a patron demand. If Nancy Drew can be tolerated cheek-by-jowl with the Newberry Award winners in the children's room, why can't the library add some of the more nontraditional Christian publications in the area of, for example, creationism?

Librarians have a professional responsibility for knowledge of bibliography in general and their own collections in particular. This means they should know the fundamentals of their patrons' literature as well. Even before asking this particular patron for her suggestions, the librarian should be pointing out to her strong examples of her point of view that may be already in the collection. Thus do the librarian and patron become firmly rooted together on common ground.

Having established a rapport, one can now address the censorship issue. Even here, one should accentuate the extent to which library policies meet patron needs. The single-minded idealist sometimes forgets that traffic in censorship runs in both directions. Anti-religious censors have strong objections to the presence of sectarian works on the shelves. Librarians must resist these efforts just as firmly as they must resist the fundamentalist's. The very zeal that protects the picture book's place on the shelves also keeps the Bible available to patrons. One has now moved directly to the library's needs. Yet again, the librarian starts with the patron's point of view, appreciating the importance of a parent's role in monitoring children's behavior and taking care not to usurp this role by deciding what things are or are not suitable for a given parent's child. Librarians have no mandate to stand *in loco parentis;* they do have the ethical mandate to make a wide variety of materials available so all parents and children can make their own choices. Just as one may respect the mother's strong stand for her beliefs, so the mother must see the need for others to stand by theirs. A procedure is then initiated for processing complaints of this nature if the patron wishes to pursue the matter further.

CONCLUSION

By following this or similar sequences, the "enemy" is given numerous opportunities to resolve things amicably by librarians taking the first step towards peace in each instance, yet without abandoning their strong sense of ethical commitment to freedom of access. While these examples are drawn from the public library field, where most of the author's experience has been, the same process will work in any setting, from academic and special librarians adjudicating between user and administration demands, to school librarians who may be blindsided on occasion by censorship from above, from school boards, and from principals.

It would be näive to believe that all censorship battles will vanish in as easy a fashion or to believe that librarians are not already using these tactics to sideline the anger of head-on disputes. The ethical issue argued here is an attitude of mind that resists confrontation and war as a first resort, an attitude that takes the responsibility for making the first move toward communication and understanding and that seeks to promote the highest level of service in the opponent's terms as much as possible. Only when that cannot be achieved without violating the Code of Ethics should one even conceive of the option of all-out battle (Burger, 1978).

The experience of converting enemy to friend, an experience that librarians do achieve on occasion, can give rise to a feeling only to be described as euphoric, if not salvific. The author exhorts his readers to go out and experience this for themselves.

REFERENCES

American Library Association. (1987). *ALA Policy Manual.* Chicago: ALA.

Burger, R. H. (1978). The Kanawha County textbook controversy: A study of communication and power. *Library Quarterly, 48*(2), 143-162.

Marsden, G. M. (1980). *Fundamentalism and American culture: The shaping of twentieth century evangelicalism, 1870-1925.* New York: Oxford University Press.

DONNA GOEHNER

Dean of Library Services
Western Illinois University
Macomb, Illinois

Ethical Aspects of the Librarian/Vendor Relationship

INTRODUCTION

If one of the aims of ethics is to define and clarify the perceptions of what constitutes the rightness or reasonableness of conduct, an obvious question is, who defines reasonable or right behavior? Individuals define reasonable behavior in their dealings with one another. However, there is a difference between describing behavior and interpreting or assessing behavior. The task ahead is to interpret and evaluate behavior between librarians and vendors, which is more difficult than description because it is necessarily subjective. Admittedly, individual and group values both play a part in how one reaches one's conclusions concerning ethics; and opinions will vary depending upon the segments of society from which comments are solicited. Because more knowledge is wanted about the ethical aspects of the librarian/vendor relationship, assessments are needed from members within those groups.

In 1987, the author conducted lengthy interviews with acquisitions librarians and library vendor representatives to determine how those individuals characterized the ethical aspects of their working relationship. The outcome of those conversations is reported in one chapter of a book entitled *Understanding the Business of Library Acquisitions* (Goehner, 1990). This paper will share information gained from responses to some of the questions posed in those 1987 interviews plus some new information. Library administrators also play an important role in determining the degree of ethical conduct that exists in relationships with vendors. By including responses from administrators to the questions previously asked of the acquisitions librarians and vendors, another perspective is added to an examination of the ethical aspects of librarian/vendor relationships.

THE INTERVIEW QUESTIONS

The interviews were conducted in the following manner. In 1987, six experienced acquisitions librarians and six successful vendors were contacted and asked to respond to the same set of questions pertaining to ethics. The librarians were from institutions of various sizes—small, medium-sized, and large. Vendor respondents were from companies that handled book orders and from companies providing subscription services. During the summer of 1989, library administrators from six states and from institutions of various sizes were contacted about participating in the survey. All individuals contacted agreed to take part in the exercise.

Since answers to questions dealing with ethical behavior are based primarily on personal opinions and value judgments, nuances in replies were more likely to be noticed in face-to-face and verbal discussions. Therefore, individual interviews were scheduled with all participants to talk about questions they had previously received through the mail. After the interviews were completed, the answers and related comments were transcribed and compiled. However, because the participants were assured anonymity prior to the interviews, their observations are not identified by name. Still, since ethical reflection means thinking about the question of what expectations others may have of one, the respondents' replies should help clarify what behavior is anticipated. The legitimacy of those expectations can be assessed to determine if, and to what degree, they are or might be accommodated.

Do Social Events Obligate a Library or Acquisitions Librarian?

Here is how the three groups responded to that question. Although everyone interviewed said that social events should not obligate librarians, the operative word is *do*. Several librarians believed there was, at least in theory, general agreement among their peers that accepting an invitation to lunch or attending a social mixer at a vendor's hospitality suite during conventions do not obligate a person in any way. One administrator's qualified response is typical of the reactions to this question: "I would like to make a distinction between the type of social event. Some of the receptions at Midwinter or annual meetings of ALA are probably different from dinners where perhaps only the institution was involved with the vendor. I would look much more warily at the small private dinner than I do the large reception." There is a point at which social entertaining does tend to create a sense of indebtedness. The likelihood of librarians allowing their decisions to be affected by social activities was believed to be directly related to the amount of money involved. The more elegant the dinner, the more lavish the social event, and the more frequent the invitations, the more likely one was to feel subtle pressure to reciprocate by placing orders with the more generous vendors. Even one of the vendors indicated that when the question is *do* rather than *should* social events obligate librarians, the answer would be, "In some cases, yes."

Nonetheless, among those interviewed there was consensus that it is a common practice for vendors and librarians to interact socially, and no one expected that behavior to change. Social activities can and often do help both parties understand each other better and can lead to improved working relationships. Vendors mentioned that a more productive discussion frequently takes place over breakfast or lunch when librarians are away from the distractions and interruptions in their work environments. To prevent matters from getting out of hand, it was suggested that vendors set reasonable fiscal guidelines for social activities and stick to them. Many corporations have established certain criteria for business entertaining that are to be adhered to by employees. Yet the values held by individuals, as well as personal motivation, determine how consistently those rules are followed.

If vendors could agree collectively to reduce the amount of money they spend on social activities, libraries might be better served. The high costs associated with entertaining are simply passed on to the library consumer in the form of lower discount rates, higher handling or transportation charges, and similar cost recovery strategies. Librarians who are genuinely interested in seeing vendors set limits on expenditures for social events were encouraged to say so. Beyond that, however, several of the respondents said that there must be a commitment to behave accordingly by declining invitations to extravagant events which could be compromising. As one vendor said during the interviews, "What fuels all this behavior is what works. If it doesn't work, it won't be continued." As long as vendors perceive that financial outlays for social events pay off, they will continue to sponsor them.

Is It Fair to Compare Your Vendor Contract with Those of Other Libraries?

One acquisitions librarian replied by saying that one of the things that contributes to keeping the library profession honest is that this type of information *is* shared even though specific names might not be used. Although the other librarians agreed, it was clear that they believed those making the comparisons should exercise care and strive for equity. Typical of the administrators' responses were these statements: "There is nothing wrong in making comparisons, but you need to be sure that you're comparing the same thing." And from another: "Yes, although you need to understand that contracts are determined by volume of business and the type of orders generated." If there are special conditions which would affect the outcome of the assessments, those qualifications should be noted. Few of the librarians thought it was unfair to discuss costs; but if there were specific stipulations negotiated with a vendor that were unique to a single institution, they questioned whether this information should be shared with other libraries. Although describing vendor contracts was not viewed as a breach of ethics by most of the librarians as long as factors figuring into the comparison were actually similar, one librarian drew the line at sharing particular discounts received from vendors.

It is apparent in the responses from vendors that attitudes toward this question differ. One vendor said that contracts between a library and a vendor were considered by his company to be private documents and that confidentiality should be maintained on both sides. The reason given for this position was that a contract is a vendor's response to a set of library-specific needs and/or requests; rarely do such specifications match library to library. Exceptions to that position were bid situations or cases where the contract is uniform for all customers.

Another vendor said it was all right for librarians to compare contracts unless there had been a specific agreement with the vendor not to reveal the details of the contract. A third vendor stated that his company's position was that a well-informed customer is a better client. Moreover, since there should be nothing to fear from an honest and fair comparison, information sharing among librarians was not viewed as a problem. Other comments made by vendors echoed the concern expressed by librarians regarding comparisons, i.e., that conditions in the respective institutions be taken into account.

What Information Should Vendors Reveal among Themselves about Libraries or Librarians? What Information Should Vendors Reveal to Librarians about Other Vendors?

Because questions three and four are very interrelated, it was more difficult for respondents to keep their answers separate. What is most interesting about all the responses to these questions is the brevity and similarity of the comments. Essentially, everyone agreed that very little information of a specific nature should be shared when vendors discuss either other libraries or other vendors in their conversations with customers or potential customers. One administrator went so far as to say that vendors should not feel they have to reveal anything about their competition or other libraries in their business dealings. Most of the individuals interviewed believed that if information were shared, it should only be nonproprietary or public information.

What Are Legitimate Promises on Both Sides?

While this question caused the most difficulty for respondents because of the word *promises*, one administrator said it was still a good question because it was thought-provoking. While this question also elicited the most discussion, the comments were more disparate and, consequently, more difficult to summarize. This was especially true because there was as much description of behavior that was disliked when legitimate promises were not kept as there was in identifying the promises. What follows, then, is a combination of what librarians expect from vendors, what vendors expect from librarians, and what business practices both groups prefer.

Vendors expect librarians to be as good as their word when they indicate the volume of orders that will be placed. Other considerations vendors appreciate are a fair mix of orders, good pre-order searching to reduce the number of duplicates and returns, and prompt payment when goods and services have been delivered as promised. Librarians should recognize a purchase order as a legal, contractual obligation representing a product or service that is going to be accepted and paid for in accordance with the vendor's terms of sale. One vendor elaborated:

> Librarians must recognize that their vendors must receive fair pay for services provided. Vendors are under tremendous strain to constantly reinvest profits back into their business, particularly regarding emerging technologies. Unrealistic demands for increasing discounts only fuel the discount gamesmanship of some vendors. In today's competitive environment we find vendors according discounts that are deemed necessary to buy a particular account. And librarians encourage this unethical happening.

One of the librarians interviewed was also uneasy about the attitude of some librarians toward the vendor's predicament. She explained:

> I am particularly concerned about delays in payment to small vendors who may already have a cash flow problem. Carrying a long overdue account may result in the failure of a small organization having limited reserves. Librarians have to be sensitive to the effects of their actions in these matters. Many librarians seem to think they deserve a lot of favors from vendors, and yet, they have little understanding of what it takes to run a business these days.

One of the administrators noted the importance of written contracts or agreements and elaborated as follows:

> I think too many things have been done with a handshake in the past. We are trying to move to written contracts whenever possible to limit the area of misunderstanding. I think some vendors resist that a bit because it holds them liable in a different way. But what I am finding is that we are getting new and different people in procurement at our institutions who are requiring us to behave in different and more businesslike ways because of external auditors. All of the publicity surrounding the costs of higher education has pushed toward much tighter cost control.

Almost all of the administrators echoed this call for putting agreements in writing. In fact, one of them declared that "anything that has to do with the business that a library does with a vendor should be in writing."

Both vendors and librarians emphasized the importance of keeping one's word. When either party does not live up to its promises, the library/vendor relationship is damaged. When a librarian negotiates a certain volume of business with a vendor (who quotes a discount based on that volume), these are considered legitimate promises.

Other ethical issues that were considered serious included defaulting on contracts; abusing policies on book returns; over-encumbering and overspending by libraries; and expecting financial support from vendors for activities unrelated to libraries. Such practices strain the library/vendor relationship and can lead not only to criticism but also to termination of the business affiliation. Numerous examples were given to illustrate the awkward position in which vendors and libraries have found themselves when the limits of probity were exceeded.

The description which follows depicts one vendor's dilemma in a case where canceling a contract was considered the appropriate course of action. Library X told Vendor Y that a certain amount of money would be spent for materials from a variety of publishers—trade, university presses, and sci-tech. Vendor Y wrote a two-year contract which included a good discount based on the volume and mix of orders projected by Library X. When the mix of orders was not at all as indicated by the library, Vendor Y's contract became unprofitable. The vendor had to decide whether to honor the contract or default and cut its losses. The company decided to fulfill its obligation for one year but to cancel at the end of the first year rather than letting the contract run the intended two-year period.

Another situation that can affect a vendor's profit margin is the extent to which librarians abuse their privileges on returns. Vendors can legitimately return books to publishers within 90-100 days. When libraries keep books longer than the publisher's return agreement specifies, the vendor again finds him- or herself in a quandary. If the late return is accepted in order to maintain a good relationship with the library, profit on the sale is forfeited. By refusing the late return, future orders from the library are jeopardized. One vendor remarked that it seemed to be that the same libraries abused this policy on a routine basis.

A related occurrence involves the return of material because of poor quality. Vendors said they ought not to be placed in the role of judges in the publishing arena and expected to evaluate the quality of material. As one vendor explained, "If inferior material is returned to us because of its content, and if the publisher will not accept the return, the vendor should not have to absorb the cost. The library should keep the book. It is not our job to see that standards of quality meet the library's expectations."

Although there were numerous examples given of ethical infringements, the practice of overspending or overextending library material budgets was selected as the last illustration to be included because it is serious and because it was reported to occur with some degree of regularity. There are libraries that not only overencumber their materials budget but also overspend their allocation. They then expect the vendor to "carry" them or bail them out. There were degrees of seriousness associated with this problem. One of the vendors described a situation where a library ordered $200,000 of processed books. After the vendor had placed, received, and processed the orders to the library's specifications, the librarian called to say there was only $100,000 in the book budget. Who was asleep at the wheel? Was it fair to expect the vendor to hold invoices for those books until the library's funds for the next fiscal year were released? Unfortunately, this was not an isolated instance of this type of behavior. The vendor's position in cases such as these was outlined in the following statement: "We have had several experiences with libraries and business offices who have overspent, promised payment, and failed to make payment over a long period of time. We have been put in a difficult situation because of such unscrupulous practices. Business officers and institutional fiscal agents should know better." One of the librarians who acknowledged that this practice was more prevalent than she liked to admit added that she did not want her library to subsidize those institutions that did not pay their bills on time.

What Do You Believe Is The Greatest Incentive to High Ethical Behavior in Organizations?

This question dealt with ethical issues of a broader nature. Most respondents had some difficulty with this question, but there was general

agreement that while the ethical tone of an organization is established
and fostered at the top, individual pride and personal integrity may be
more influential in determining how ethically an organization operates.
As one library director explained, "It seems to me that ethical behavior
is learned. You watch how people behave when you are young, and if
you observe ethical behavior, you will tend to follow that example."
And another director observed, "We tend to give out punishment for
unethical behavior, but I can't think of any rewards for high ethical
behavior either in our professional associations or any place else in
society." A third library administrator said she would urge keeping in
mind whether the behavior and decision will bear close public scrutiny.

Management has to assume responsibility for defining and maintaining the value system within an organization. Among the values cited
as prerequisites for high ethical behavior were fairness, honesty, and
respect for others. If high standards are demanded and practiced by
those in positions of leadership, other people in the organization will
be more inclined to follow suit. In the words of one of the librarians,
proper behavior is more likely to occur "just by knowing that ethical
behavior is what the other person expects, by letting each other know
when these expectations have not been achieved, and by indicating how
severe the lapse was judged to be." Another respondent said that a
good reputation is built up over a long period of time and that consistency
in doing the right thing is how respect is earned. Avoiding short-term,
quick-fix solutions to problems was considered a good approach to
establishing the necessary climate for success. As one individual noted,
perhaps the greatest incentive to high ethical behavior in organizations
is "the clear indication that unethical behavior is intolerable. Moreover,
the environment should be such that others within the organization
would be shocked if unethical acts had been committed."

What Do You Believe Is The Major Cause for Ethical Lapses?

As might be expected from previous answers, one reason given for
ethical lapses was the failure within the organization to have clearly
defined and communicated the expectation for high ethical behavior.
Lack of concern on the part of leadership does make a difference in
how people behave. If an executive officer does not exercise internal
control by telling staff that ethics is an important issue, the business
practices of some employees may deteriorate. An organization is ultimately defined by the caliber of people it employs, not by mission
statements or advertising claims. Therefore, if the ethical conduct of
an individual degenerates, the good name of the organization also
suffers. When the bottom line becomes the prime consideration for

vendors, the company is jeopardizing its reputation. Based on those observations, it was not surprising that most respondents said that greed was the major cause of ethical lapses. This reason would apply more to vendors than librarians in the previous context; yet librarians put themselves in a similar position when they ask vendors for donations knowing that the vendor's interest will not be served. For instance, how does a vendor benefit when he agrees to make a donation toward a university's fund drive for a new field house? Vendors reported cases even more flagrant. Some university development officers telephone companies having major accounts with their institution and ask for substantial donations to their development programs. The implication is that if the company does not contribute, the institution might select another vendor for services being provided by the present supplier.

While activities centering around money were mentioned most often as ones which can lead to questionable conduct, other causes for ethical lapses were identified. They included näivete, thoughtlessness, egotism, and exploitation. One respondent said a major cause for ethical lapses was simply plain ignorance of what should be the standard of behavior. Others mentioned as causes lack of good judgment, the desire to take advantage of a situation, and a feeling of dissatisfaction with the organization. However, the majority of respondents thought that vendors and librarians were, for the most part, a very ethical group of people. Commenting on the conduct of both parties, one librarian observed: "I think in some ways we are to be complimented because the number of cases we see that involve unethical behavior on the part of librarians or vendors is minimal."

CONCLUSION

It would be possible to end this presentation with the above positive statement. However, there are a few concluding remarks that should be mentioned. Each person was asked if there were other comments they would like to make pertaining either to ethics or to the relationship between librarians and vendors that were not covered in the previous questions. Several of the respondents noted that few library schools teach students much about the publishing world, the acquisitions process, or how to be a good consumer. Many librarians accept positions in an acquisitions department with little firsthand knowledge of basic book-keeping practices, contract negotiations, financial reports, or accounting principles. They know even less about how vendors operate. This void in their program of studies has to be filled on the job and can result in a less-than-optimum business relationship with seasoned vendors. However, there was the perception that librarians were becoming more businesslike in their approach to acquisitions. As fiscal agents for their institutions, librarians are responsible for monitoring the expenditure of many thousands of dollars. To build quality collections, they should make every effort to ensure that they are acquiring the most appropriate material money can buy. They should be able to provide valid reasons for their choices and indicate how the selections they make contribute to quality and value for library users. One of the vendors went so far as to say that he thought it was unethical for a librarian to spend large sums of money for books and not expect to be held accountable for where the money was spent or how good a value was received. With more access to the products of automation, there is the potential for better management information to monitor the performance of vendors and librarians. While this could lead to more scrutiny and more competitiveness, the general consensus of respondents was that having better data is essential in evaluating effectiveness.

Finally, joint decision-making regarding appropriate conduct can be successful only if both parties are frank in their assessments and if they have entered into the discussions with good intentions. As expected behaviors are communicated openly and candidly, both librarians and vendors will gain a better understanding of how to interact more ethically and effectively in their business dealings with one another. The odds of seeing eye to eye will surely be improved through such dialogue.

REFERENCE

Goehner, D. (1990). Vendor-library reltions: The ethics of working with vendors. In K. A. Schmidt (Ed.), *Understanding the business of library acquisitions* (pp. 137-51). Chicago: ALA.

ROBERT HAUPTMAN

Associate Professor
Learning Resources Services
St. Cloud State University
St. Cloud, Minnesota

Five Assaults on Our Integrity

[*Author's note:* This essay is for Bill Katz, with thanks.]

INTRODUCTION

Librarians, information disseminators, and information scientists have only infrequently concerned themselves with ethical matters. A search of the early literature reveals virtually nothing on the topic and what there is deals with etiquette and decorum rather than ethics. In 1976, the author published the results of that now infamous bomb experiment (Hauptman, 1976). Subsequently, there have appeared two books, *Professional Ethics and Librarians* (Lindsey & Prentice, 1985) and *Ethical Challenges in Librarianship* (Hauptman, 1988); a number of issues of journals exclusively devoted to the topic; and, closer to the present, a burgeoning of periodical articles on every conceivable topic. Furthermore, there have been many seminars, symposia, sections, and conferences at Rutgers University, the University of North Texas, the American Association of Law Librarians, the American Library Association, and now at the Allerton Institute. Concurrently, the social responsibilities movement has attempted to counter the mythic conception of the library's neutrality in order to ameliorate social conditions, but its influence has been negligible. Long ago, Samuel Rothstein (1968) called for the creation of an ethos out of which librarians could function. Later, Stephen Almagno (1989) articulated the need for a new ethic, something akin to the new perspective that Hans Jonas (1984) insists is now required to cope with the problems of our technological age.

Sometimes, discussions of ethics and librarianship emphasize theoretical matters; more often, they are hortatory in nature, citing practical examples in order to inspire actions that will bring glory to the profession. This paper comments on five intellectual concepts—confidentiality, intellectual freedom, censorship, honesty, and malpractice—by describing some often bizarre cases that have come to the author's attention.

CONFIDENTIALITY

Confidentiality is the hallmark of the traditional professions and it is easy to understand why. If trust in one's doctor, lawyer, or clergyman is misplaced, then one will be chary of disclosing personal matters to these people in the future. Information disseminators are in an analogous position. Additionally, forty-one states now have confidentiality statutes in place in order to protect the confidences of library patrons.

More than ten years ago, the Federal Bureau of Investigation began its Library Awareness Program, which ostensibly protects this country's freedom by monitoring Soviet spies' access to information, especially in scientific and technical libraries in the New York metropolitan area. At least, these are the officially stated parameters. Librarians refused to cooperate because to reveal any information about patrons is a breach of confidentiality. What is interesting is that this case really does create an ethical dilemma for both parties. And they both solve it in the same way: by ignoring the opposite side of the equation. The FBI investigators, who certainly do respect the concept of confidentiality in their own work, set it aside here for a higher good; the librarians, who generally favor American democracy, simply do not consider the FBI perspective.

One could be more sympathetic to the Bureau's position if there really did appear to be some threat to national security and if the librarians' cooperation really could help, and one could be more sympathetic to the librarians' stance if confidentiality were not breached in other areas. Circulation records continue to identify users by name, especially in systems that are no longer operative but that have not entirely eliminated the earlier records. Interlibrary loan procedures often advertise the connection between user and material. Online searchers may allow search forms to lie around so that anyone can glance at them. These same forms are stored for future reference and so anyone with access to the files has access to the patrons' identities. Finally, when printing offline, it is not unusual to use the patron's name as an indicator; thus, everyone along the communication trail can easily connect the patron with his or her information needs.

In response to the author's query, Milt Ahlerich, Assistant Director of the FBI's Office of Congressional and Public Affairs, indicated that the Bureau intended to persevere with its program. His response was couched in precisely the same words that Gerald Shields quoted earlier in these proceedings: Although librarians do not have to cooperate, ". . . we are confident that they will help if the program is explained to them properly" (M. Ahlerich, personal communication, January 13, 1989). Yet, virtually all individuals, organizations (ARL, SLA, ALA, ACLU), and Congress roundly deplore the program. In fact, California Congressman Don Edwards (1989) of the House Judiciary Committee has been inspired by this brouhaha to call for stricter limits on the FBI's power and a reexamination of those laws relating to information access and dissemination including the Freedom of Information and Paperwork Reduction Acts. As Edwards notes, "Given the limited results compared with the confusion and concern that it has generated, I think the Bureau would be best served by strictly limiting the program or curtailing it altogether" (Mitgang, 1988, p. C22).

INTELLECTUAL FREEDOM

In a democracy, intellectual freedom is the most basic of individual rights. Even those people who live in totalitarian countries such as Albania or North Korea and who have been brainwashed into ostensibly believing the party line may hold other ideas that they do not articulate. In a democracy, it is an inherent right to be able to hold divergent ideas and to articulate them as well. Many years ago, when the author was lucky enough to live in the snowy Vermont woods with nothing to do except read and write, he happened one day to pick up an extremely intelligent hitchhiker, a law student who believed that the solution to humanity's problems lay in theoretical Marxism as implemented under communism in the Soviet Union. After going around in circles for many hours, this author finally said that, in order to achieve its ends, the Soviet system apparently requires an abrogation of basic human rights. The hitchhiker immediately agreed, insisting that that is a sacrifice well worth making. He was wrong. Once a human being has the basic necessities (food and housing), there is nothing more important than individual rights, and the most important of these allows one to hold divergent beliefs and to articulate them as one sees fit.

There exists a nonpartisan state agency (which must remain anonymous in order to protect the informant) that drafts bills, analyzes fiscal matters, and renders legal opinions for the state legislature. In August of 1987, an article appeared in the weekly state law journal (the journal of record) questioning the nonpartisan attitude of the executive director of the agency in relation to a conflict of interest case. His party affiliation was identified. As the informant put it, he (the director) "went nuts."

His overseeing commission complained to the journal's editor who, instead of being mollified, responded in print with further accusations. The end result of all of this was that the director canceled the subscriptions to the state law journals—all four of them! The librarians and even the lawyers in the agency fought against this ludicrous decision, but lost. Now, more than two years later, the agency still does not have a subscription to this extremely important source of germane information. Here is my informant's eloquent peroration:

> As you can imagine, this created quite a dilemma for me personally and professionally. I have always been strongly anti-censorship regardless of the circumstances and regardless of the so-called reasons for censorship. The particular circumstances in this case were so silly and blown out of proportion that it was an embarrassment. Professionally, of course, the Journal is a necessity for "my" patrons and has created a real hardship for them. I do think, however, that I did what I could, as did the lawyers here. The E.D. has lost a lot of respect among people here for his pettiness and willingness to sacrifice the quality and accuracy of work done in the agency because of a perceived slight. (Informant, personal communication, August 30, 1989)

CENSORSHIP

Censorship is a specific subset of intellectual freedom, the attempt on the part of an individual or group to impede another person's access to information, which comes in diverse formats including print, cinema, painting, and sculpture. As John Swan (1986) so neatly puts it, "The suppression of any idea can be dangerous to the flow of all ideas" (p. 10).

Anyone who has ever visited Sienna will never forget the alternating black and white stone blocks that sheath the Cathedral, nor the Palazzo Pubblico in which one will find Simone Martini's great fresco, *Guido Riccio da Fogliano at the Siege of Montemassi*. This ten-by-thirty-foot painting is an extremely important work, a transition piece marking the change from the medieval to the early Renaissance style. It is often reproduced in art history books and it has come to be viewed as a symbol of the city of Sienna. In 1977, Gordon Moran and Michael Mallory published an article in *Paragone* questioning the ascription of this painting to Martini. With only one exception, the Italian art establishment attacked Moran viciously, calling him a monomaniac, a paranoid, and, of course, a CIA agent. It is not necessary here to discuss in detail the precise nature of this controversy, the "enigma of the century" or "the case of the century," as it has been termed (Moran & Mallory, 1986, p. 123).

Let it suffice to indicate that in 1328, Martini purportedly painted the work; in 1333, Guido Riccio, a mercenary in the service of Sienna, left the city in disgrace, and Moran claims that the painting would have been defaced; in about 1352, Guido Riccio returned and the work could have been painted at this time as a memorial to him, except that dead men do not paint frescos: Martini had died eight years earlier, in 1344. Most convincing is that the fresco is never mentioned in the literature prior to 1700 (Raynor, 1984). This case has had wide coverage in the popular press, and *Newsweek* and *Connoisseur* have given it objective and even sympathetic readings (Young & Widmann, 1985; Raynor, 1984).

But what has all of this has to do with ethics? In 1970, the Art History Institute in Florence began indexing journal articles for its authors' catalog. The librarians claimed to cover more journals than are indexed in RILA (*Repertoire International de la Litterature de l'Art*), the primary hard copy index and online database for art history. In 1980, because of budgetary constraints, a selectivity policy was implemented and some less important journals were eliminated. Between 1980 and 1982, four articles were published that sided with Max Seidel, an affiliate of the Institute who is diametrically opposed to the Moran/ Mallory thesis. All of these were indexed in the author catalog. During the same period, five articles appeared that agreed with Moran. None of these was included in the author catalog, despite the fact that the journals involved often did fulfill the criteria set up in order to differentiate the important from the unimportant periodicals (Moran & Mallory, 1986). More unpleasant surprises were to follow. An offprint of an article that Moran presented to the Institute was ignored, and when he inquired about it, he was treated shabbily (Moran, 1987). The list of unimportant journals was kept a secret for many years. The February 1984 *News from RILA* was held back from scholars (who come from all over the world to do research there) because it contained a lead article describing the controversy and abstracts of twelve essays that concur with the Moran/Mallory thesis (Wohl, 1984). The most disconcerting aspect of this case is that when Moran and Mallory discovered some mistranscriptions in Seidel's subsequently published articles and attempted to make corrections in the appropriate journals, they were continually met with rejections by peer reviewers and editors (G. Moran, personal communication, January 20, 1989). If the use of the term *conspiracy* to describe much of this sounds too harsh at this point, readers may change their minds after reading the following section concerning the honesty of information creators.

HONESTY

On Truth, Lies, and Intellectual Embezzlement

The concern here is not with librarians, but rather with those humanists, social scientists, and scientists who do research and publish the results, the creators of the information that is collected and disseminated. In "Untruth or Consequences" (Swan, 1986) and more recently in *The Freedom to Lie* (Swan & Peattie, 1989), John Swan makes a surprisingly strong case for collecting false or incorrect information. He claims that selectors and collection developers must refuse to differentiate the true from the false. It is hardly necessary to cite Ptolemy, Galileo, or Semmelweis in order to prove that the past's truths are the present's falsehoods, and vice-versa. For collectors, intellectual freedom and the "toleration for the detestable" are more important than truth. But this is decidedly not the case for those people who do research, whose goal is invariably the discovery of truth. Few researchers begin their work with the *a priori* objective of dissimulating, but skewing, fudging, and outright fraud are far more prevalent than most researchers in all fields care to admit.

Judith Serebnick and Stephen Harter (1990) queried editors of scholarly journals concerning the honesty of authors. They posed twenty-two situations concerning, for example, negligence, falsification, multiple submissions, multiple authors, and previous publications. What they found was that, sometimes, the individual editor is the key to a journal's ethical practices. ". . . The commonality of the editors' responses suggests that opinions about ethics among journal editors in a discipline [may] follow recognizable patterns" (p. 116). Byron J. Bailey (1989) of the University of Texas, speaking at the American Medical Association's Peer Review Congress in the Spring of 1989, discovered that of 1,000 authors whose writings he examined, 228 (more than one quarter) republished the same material over and over again, for a total of 938 publications. Journal editors are also guilty of manipulation. They tend to favor senior researchers at prestigious institutions. And, of course, they prefer material that jibes with theories that happen to be in vogue at the time of submission. Unfashionable theories or explanations often get short shrift.

Most culpable, though, are the peer reviewers, those colleagues who read and pass judgement on the articles submitted to periodical editors. Naturally, many of these referees are honest, objective, and diligent, but a surprising number are not. Do they plagiarize? They do indeed: Some time ago, during the superconductivity brouhaha, Paul C. W. Chu of the University of Houston submitted an article that contained an incorrect element. Shortly thereafter, the incorrect element was leaked to Chu's competitors by the referees. No one knows whether Chu purposely cited the incorrect element in order to protect his discovery (Coughlin, 1989).

Peer Review and Quality Control

Does the peer review process control the quality of publications? Joseph M. Garfunkel of the *Journal of Pediatrics* resubmitted twenty-five accepted papers to a new set of peer reviewers. Eight of the twenty-five articles were rejected on this second reading (Garfunkel et al., 1989). Vincent A. Fulginiti of the *American Journal of Diseases of Children* resubmitted all 1988 accepted manuscripts to a new set of referees. Complete data are not yet available, but of the decisions made thus far, 43 percent of the originally accepted articles were rejected. As Fulginiti astutely observes, ". . . referees have widely divergent views on the value, substance, and acceptability of original research and observations. The fate of a given manuscript appears heavily dependent on the referee(s) selected and the weight given that opinion by the editorial board and editor" (Fulginiti et al., 1989, p. 16).

Why are papers rejected? Two years ago, Erdem I. Cantekin of the University of Pittsburgh Medical School reported "negative results from a clinical trial" concerning the efficacy of a widely prescribed medication. This article has been repeatedly rejected by reviewers and editors because of the influence of persons who have conflicts of interest with the findings. That the results have not been disseminated ". . . may have directly influenced the public health in this country" (Cantekin et al., 1989, p. 20). This is especially disconcerting since the case has been widely discussed on television news programs (*CBS, CNN*), in the press (*The New York Times, The Washington Post*), and in scholarly journals such as *The Economist, The Lancet,* and *Nature,* but to no avail since the paper has not yet appeared in the appropriate journals.

Errors that manage to get into the literature can be corrected. Eugene Garfield (1989) of the Institute for Scientific Information shows through citation analysis that once fraudulent data is recognized, it will slowly be purged. Lois Ann Colaianni of the National Library of Medicine indicates that workers often discover errors when indexing MEDLINE, the medical database. These are sometimes corrected in the database with the editor's permission before an erratum notice is published in the journal. This is extremely important because in 1987, almost 2500 errors were noted, including incorrect dosages for medicines (Colaianni et al., 1989).

If the peer review process is not especially good at catching fraudulence and error, it is extremely effective at stifling innovation.

David Horrobin, editor of *Medical Hypotheses,* the only journal devoted entirely to ideas in medicine, observes that virtually all of the 2,000 papers that have appeared in his periodical had been repeatedly rejected by other journals. His incisive conclusion should be carefully noted: "Patients are ill-served by a review system that penalizes innovation and encourages conformity" (Horrobin, 1989, p. 24). This, too, is a conspiracy of sorts, one that has detrimental effects on the production of useful knowledge.

MALPRACTICE

Four major areas of concern have thus far been discussed: confidentiality, intellectual freedom, censorship, and honesty. Now, what occurs when a mistake is made that yields incorrect or unacceptable results? Errors are punished in a way that is most painful—through the error-maker's pocketbook. If technology, especially CD-ROM, has been the catchword for the 1980s, then information liability will be the key term for the 1990s. As Anne Mintz (1984) points out, database producers, indexers, packagers, disseminators, communicators, and searchers are all responsible for the accuracy of the information provided. Thus it is now necessary to protect oneself with disclaimers, legally binding contracts, education, values inculcation, and competency. Suits that may arise from information malpractice are no longer hypothetical. In 1984, the Supreme Court awarded Greenmoss Builders of Burlington, Vermont $350,000, primarily in punitive damages, because Dun and Bradstreet incorrectly indicated in its database that the company was bankrupt. As John H. Everett (1989) wisely observes, "Hiding behind the image of the poor, but sincerely helpful, librarian won't be an effective deterrent for much longer" (p. 66).

It is hoped that the preceding comments will be useful in helping to formulate an ethos, a new ethic, out of which information disseminators can function effectively.

REFERENCES

Almagno, R. S. (1989). Rilke's advice. *Catholic Library World, 60*(4), 150-152.
Bailey, B. J. (1989). Duplicate publication in otolaryngology—head and neck surgery. In D. Rennie (Ed.), *Guarding the guardians: Research on peer review* (Abstracts of the 1st International Congress on Peer Review in Biomedical Publications, 10-12 May 1989) (pp. 12-13). Chicago: American Medical Association.
Cantekin, E. I.; McGuire, T. W.; & Potter, R. L. (1989). Biomedical information, peer reviews, and conflict of interest as they influence public health. In D. Rennie (Ed.), *Guarding the guardians: Research on peer review* (Abstracts of the 1st International Congress on Peer Review in Biomedical Publications, 10-12 May 1989) (pp. 19-20). Chicago: AMA.

Colaianni, L. A.; Kotzin, S.; & Selinger, N. (1989). Online identification of published errata notices. In D. Rennie (Ed.), *Guarding the guardians: Research on peer review* (Abstracts of the 1st International Congress on Peer Review in Biomedical Publications, 10-12 May 1989) (p. 23). Chicago: AMA.

Coughlin, E. K. (1989). Concerns about fraud, editorial bias prompt scrutiny of journal practices. *The Chronicle of Higher Education*, (15 February), A4-A7.

Edwards, D. (1989). Government information controls threaten academic freedom. *Thought and Action, V*(1), 87-88.

Everett, J. H. (1989). Independent information professionals and the question of malpractice liability. *ONLINE* (May), 65-70.

Fulginiti, V. A.; Corrigan, J. J.; Allen, H. D.; Bedrick, A.; Quane, J. M.; & Martin, L. C. (1989). Comparative review before and after acceptance of a manuscript. In D. Rennie (Ed.), *Guarding the guardians: Research on peer review* (Abstracts of the 1st International Congress on Peer Review in Biomedical Publications, 10-12 May 1989) (pp. 15-16). Chicago: AMA.

Garfield, E. (1989). The impact of scientific fraud. In D. Rennie (Ed.), *Guarding the guardians: Research on peer review* (Abstracts of the 1st International Congress on Peer Review in Biomedical Publications, 10-12 May 1989) (p. 23). Chicago: AMA.

Garfunkel, J. M.; Ulshen, M. H.; Hamrick, H. A.; & Lawson, E. E. (1989). Re-review of accepted manuscripts. In D. Rennie (Ed.), *Guarding the guardians: Research on peer review* (Abstracts of the 1st International Congress on Peer Review in Biomedical Publications, 10-12 May 1989) (p. 15). Chicago: AMA.

Hauptman, R. (1976). Professionalism or culpability? An experiment in ethics. *Wilson Library Bulletin, 5*(8), 626-627.

Hauptman, R. (1988). *Ethical challenges in librarianship*. Phoenix, AZ: Oryx.

Horrobin, D. (1989). The philosophical basis of peer review. In D. Rennie (Ed.), *Guarding the guardians: Research on peer review* (Abstracts of the 1st International Congress on Peer Review in Biomedical Publications, 10-12 May 1989)(p. 24). Chicago: AMA.

Jonas, H. (1984). *The imperative of responsibility: In search of an ethics for the technological age*. Chicago: University of Chicago Press.

Lindsey, J. A., & Prentice, A. E. (1985). *Professional ethics and librarians*. Phoenix, AZ: Oryx.

Mintz, A. P. (1984). Information practice and malpractice . . . Do we need malpractice insurance? *ONLINE, 8*(4), 20-26.

Mitgang, H. (1988, August 31). Book notes. *The New York Times*, p. C22.

Moran, G. (1987). Biting the hand that feeds. [Letter to the editor]. *Library Journal, 112*(5), 6.

Moran, G., & Mallory, M. (1986). Selective card cataloging (or in-house screening of periodical indexing) of art history articles in authors' files and the potential effect of this "selectivity" on the bibliographical entries relating to specific art historical problems: A case study. In K. Wynia (Ed.), *Art periodicals* (Papers of the 2nd European Conference of the Art Libraries of IFLA, Amsterdam, 13-17 October 1986)(pp. 123-132). Amsterdam: Bibliothek Vrije Universiteit.

Raynor, W. (1984). The case against Simone. *Connoisseur* (October), 60-71.

Rothstein, S. (1968). In search of ourselves. *Library Journal, 93*(2), 156-157.

Serebnick, J., & Harter, S. (1990). Ethical practices in journal publishing: A study of library and information science periodicals. *Library Quarterly, 60*(2), 91-119.

Swan, J. C. (1986). Untruth or consequences. *Library Journal, 111*(12), 44-52.

Swan, J. C., & Peattie, N. (1989). *The freedom to lie: A debate about democracy*. Jefferson, NC: McFarland.

Wohl, A. S. (1984, February). In Sienna, an old masterpiece challenged, a new one discovered. *News from RILA*, pp. 1, 4, 5, 11.

Young, J., & Widmann, L. (1985, 4 February). Italy's great fresco fracas. *Newsweek*, p. 45.

SAMUEL F. MORRISON

First Deputy Commissioner and Chief Librarian
Chicago Public Library

The Ethics of Access:
Towards an Equal Slice of the Pie

INTRODUCTION

The regard for ethics for a period of time drifted away from the lofty logic of Socrates and religious seminaries, and became a topic avoided by the political arena and forgotten by society. However, in recent times, ethics has returned to the forefront, an issue that is addressed by the media, in various publications, and at many symposiums and conferences and by politicians. In other words, it is again currently a "hot" topic. The ethical standing and responsibility of professions such as librarianship, which have an impact upon the community at large, are significant and worthy of this attention.

Ethics is a system of moral principles and of values relating to the rightness and wrongness of certain actions. When two diametrically opposed obligations conflict with one another, an ethical dilemma occurs. It is settled only by weighing and evaluating the importance of the conflicting obligations. The moral conviction of a democratic society supportive of freedom of information versus the welfare of that public might well be an example of two opposing obligations. Equal access to information by the people versus the provision of relevant and friendly information is another wordset of potentially opposing obligations. The free library for the good of the public versus quality library services is also a contender. It is not so opposing if one considers the statement of Alphonse Trezza (1986) during his tenure with the National Commission on Library and Information Services (NCLIS): "The commitment to public good requires the library to constantly improve quality of services, the effective use of technology, and the efficiency of the operation" (p. 52). Providing access and fulfilling the needs of the majority versus providing access and fulfilling the needs of the minority is yet another opposing set. If one adds the words "equal opportunity" then the impact of this statement upon the library is significant.

As a public administrator, the author's concern is with the responsibility of the public library to provide meaningful and quality access to minorities. For the purposes of this paper, minorities are identified as the ethnic and racial minority groups. U. S. Immigration Service statistics project that minorities will comprise 33 percent of the population by the year 2000. Currently, minority groups comprise 23 percent and up to 50 percent of the population of the larger cities of the U. S. The three largest groups of this growing minority population are Hispanic, Asian, and African-American. The highest percentages are found in New York, Los Angeles, Miami, and Chicago. In the city of Chicago, projections by the Department of Planning show the Hispanic and Asian communities as the fastest-growing components of the population, rising from 14 percent of the population in 1980 to 21 percent by 2000; coincidentally or not, the poverty rate is projected to increase by 5 percent. In all age brackets, Asian and Hispanic groups will experience significant increases, up from 20 percent to 166 percent among senior citizens, while the white population will experience decreases in all but the "over 80" category.

What are some of the obligations of libraries in giving serious consideration to minority access? First, a library is obliged to determine who the groups are, their social, cultural and demographic characteristics, and their information needs. This can be part of a community survey, needs assessment, or ascertained from existing data such as census reports and local, state and federal agency documents. Second, the library is obligated to plan for the inclusion of the needs of minority groups in its overall program of service. Prioritized and measurable goals can then be identified and implemented. Third, the library should set current and projected funding priorities for specialized services to minority groups. The availability of "soft" money for such services has dwindled so that mainstreaming should be the order of the day.

Before considering funding and overcoming budgetary constraints, some of the other major considerations involved in the responsibility of libraries to provide access to minorities need to be addressed. In this era of reduced library funding, especially at the federal level, the ethics of minority access demands serious consideration.

THE "BIG FOUR" LIBRARY OPERATIONS

Meaningful, quality-oriented access requires the inclusion of minority considerations in all aspects of library operations. Foremost among these are the big four: Collections, Staffing, Programming, and Facilities. Experience and research have shown that there are differences between library needs of a vast portion of minority groups and the needs of the heretofore "typical" library user. Ethical considerations require that these differences, whether cultural, educational or social, be taken into account when proportioning library resources. This paper will touch upon some of the barriers or obstacles that must be overcome in providing meaningful, quality access and note some of the current initiatives underway at the Chicago Public Library (CPL).

Collection Access

Libraries have recognized for some time that there are distinct barriers which impede access to use of the collection. Minority groups in particular experience to a higher degree the limitations of cultural, educational, and language barriers. The ethics of access dictate that a means be implemented which will prevent minorities from becoming victims of those barriers.

Culturally, many have not used libraries as a primary or secondary source of information. Indeed, many may not have experienced the "public library" nor developed the reading habit as part of the socialization process. These groups, once identified, will have to be introduced to libraries through public awareness and community outreach efforts. To decrease the educational and language barriers, the library may have to increase its offering of English as a Second Language (ESL) and other classes and provide basic literacy training. A collection must be developed that takes these and other significant issues into consideration when plans are being developed and dollars allocated. Formats or media types may have to be expanded, deleted, or maintained. The acquisition of foreign language materials and the turnaround time for receiving, processing, and shelving these materials are critical. The inadequacy of current cataloguing and processing procedures and devices cripples the best intentions of the selection process. Far too often, what ends up on the browsing shelves is not representative of what is in the receiving and work rooms. Access to information about and for minorities is handicapped. For the staff of CPL, knowing the community means knowing which of the collected materials, in 120 different languages, to focus upon and extensively collect. The availability from major vendors, the handling of non-roman alphabets, the integration of foreign language/multicultural materials throughout a multibranch system, or the separation or regionalizing of library materials are strategic decisions to be made.

Cooperative efforts, especially where the dollar is an issue (and where isn't it!) seem to work well. For instance, Project ASIA was originally supported by LSCA funds and the book budget contributions of its participating libraries in California. Community outreach was conducted and the project staff selected, acquired, and catalogued books in four Asian languages for its participants.

Staffing

It is important to effective service to minority groups that staff are people-oriented, possess good communication skills, and are knowledgeable about the literature, aware of trends, familiar with patron needs, quality-minded, able to manage, and so on. These characteristics should sound very familiar to all library managers. The staff should also be familiar with the institutional barriers that can impede access to information. The information needs of those in low-income areas and the non-English speaking can be a far cry from what is taught in Reference 101. Librarians have to recognize the socioeconomic and educational distinctions within a given minority group and consequently their diverse informational needs. Staff awareness and sensitivity for institutional barriers can extend from knowing when a given collection is inadequate for a patron and thereby providing the appropriate referral; or when a person is at a loss in attempting to recognize, let alone use, the catalog, follow the Library of Congress classification scheme, or simply read. The responsive library and staff will proceed to establish workable measures to reduce institutional barriers. The establishment of staff advisory committees that serve as resources for the development and administration of policies, activities, collections, and programs affecting minorities is one approach for creating and passing on the awareness alluded to previously.

In some instances, there are needs for bilingual staff. At CPL, staff working in primarily Hispanic communities are encouraged and supported in their efforts to learn Spanish. As a result of LSCA funding, there have been language classes offered for staff on library time. CPL has also initiated a joint program with Rosary College whereby staff with bachelor's degrees can work full time and complete M.L.S. degree requirements within two years. This staff development program is designed to increase the number of librarians available systemwide and therefore for the new central library—the Harold Washington Library Center (scheduled for completion in 1991)—as well as to enlarge the diminishing pool of minority librarians. In the city's personnel department, a training program is offered for all city employees on multicultural adaptation; one is targeted for managers and another for peer groups.

One of CPL's four district chief librarians provides the following insight: Attitudes of staff in communities that are experiencing changes in makeup are often difficult to orient. In one branch, the community makeup is moving away from a white-collar, all-white neighborhood to one of blue-collar, Hispanic predominance. The unit head is expected to orientate her middle-aged white clerical staff so that they maintain the same level of quality service for the newer residents of the community as they have given in the past. This is a considerable task under some conditions, but especially so in this case when the observation is made that the branch head herself is making plans to move her personal residence out of that community.

CPL actively recruits bilingual staff, who are assigned to those areas of the library needing their skills the most. However, should the rightness and wrongness of shaping the career track of bilingual and minority staff be considered? Are there other skills, language fluency aside, that are being overlooked which would enhance the employee's value to the organization? Does the library have an obligation to assign qualified minority professional staff to communities whose makeup and patrons are not those of the librarian's ethnic or racial type? Is the library's "commitment to quality library services" kept in mind at personnel evaluation time? Are supervisors wise to the differences in work habits caused by cultural differences versus "poor" work habits?

Programming

Another major area where the ethics of access comes into play is library programming. Is a proportionate share of programming planned with minorities in mind? Do the program participants, themes, and topics reflect the ethnicity of the community? Do they go beyond simply a linguistic translation of traditional programming?

In conjunction with the program design element, marketing needs must be considered. The need arises for effective communication. This may mean bilingual press releases, public service announcements, and any other means identified by community outreach that serve to inform staff of the best communication vehicles and channels for a given minority group and community. For instance, in some Arab neighborhoods, mosques and grocery stores with Arab proprietors are the current and most-used source for community information. For other groups it may be the church or the social center. The two underlying purposes of programming are to increase library use and to promote cultural awareness. For minority groups as with any other group, relevance, i.e., meaningful access, is the key.

Facilities

The last of the big four of library operations is facilities. Here is where, in a number of instances, the proportionate share is not met. It is usually in minority communities that one finds a predominance of storefronts and smaller library facilities. In many instances, groups have not been empowered to demand better facilities, nor are they aware of the political process for obtaining improvements. Once the groups grow large enough and become more acquainted with the process for improvement, the demands are made. But why wait until then? If the concern for minority access and ethical considerations is incorporated in the library's capital improvement plans, then adequate facilities become a part of the library's ongoing program. CPL recently opened an 18,000 square-foot branch in the heart of a large Hispanic community. This facility is one of the many included in the library's five-year plan for branch renovation and construction within the 84-agency library. A storefront library in Chicago's Chinatown is being replaced with a new construction more suitable for the collection and community served in Chinatown.

FUNDING

There is, of course, the underlying support of all the foregoing aspects of library operations: funding. Funding is where the proportionate share of the pie really begins. This involves conscientious planning after needs have been determined. Breaking away from the traditional modes and providing for the special needs of minority groups in the budget process have, in the recent past, been reactive. Libraries were compelled by the force of local demand to respond to groups such as African-Americans and Hispanics. A library should and must in its planning stages be aware of changing communities and become proactive. Is there a new group entering the scene to which the library should be responding, such as the Asian Indian population, before the group requests an audience with the board of directors or trustees?

"Towards an equal slice of the pie" means the implementation of a plan. It should contain the elements of a contingency plan as well as long-range considerations. It should include available and potentially available funding sources. When the budget is tight, the first inclination usually is to postpone doing anything. However, this is problematic. Resources must be tapped, whether public or private. Again, being in touch with the community may reveal certain power brokers previously unknown.

Another source of funds or means for adding services is the use of creative partnerships. Other agencies or institutions may be willing to pool resources and work with the library in joint sponsorship of an effort that neither alone could provide. In addition to that noted previously, a well-known example is the joint offering of English as a Second Language classes as an effort between the public library and the local adult education providers. Museums housing and exhibiting the art or history of a given minority might also be considered. Searching for these extra public and private dollars takes some ingenuity and time. At the same time, one must be prepared; the funding of services not provided previously or the funding of program ideas that do not ring a familiar bell of "traditional" will require that administrators be equipped with a salable and workable plan. This is especially true if the plan suggests the eventuality of cutting or minimizing some existing traditional service or program.

With regard to the corporate budget, specific allocations based upon the library mission, goals, and financial plan should be made during the budget process. These may be small, for example, the hiring of a bilingual specialist, a beginning "towards an equal slice of the pie."

CONCLUSION

The ethical issue of information service and access for minority groups is not going away. It has been and will continue to be a part of life in an ever-changing American society. In addition to the emerging and growing ethnic and racial groups are other minorities yet to be considered in a consistent and real way: the physically and mentally disabled, the institutionalized, the burgeoning senior citizen group, and the homeless, to name but a few of the statistically obvious.

It is impossible to provide a single approach to responding to the need for equal opportunity of access by minorities, and it is just as improbable that a Bandaid or other "quick fix" will address the need in a quality way.

The quality of service requested by minority groups is equivalent to that required by the majority, while the lesson of learning about and using the library is one for librarians and administrators. Are not librarians and administrators the minority when it comes to that segment of the population that can be defined as possessing skill and ease of access to library services and information? Thus, that minority is the one that must adapt. The opportunities found within a community must be identified and communicated; otherwise, the uniqueness and richness of our diversified and multicultural communities might not remain a treasure of libraries to keep.

ACKNOWLEDGEMENTS

It is with sincerest appreciation that the author acknowledges the contributions of the following CPL staff: Dr. Alice Scott, Assistant Commissioner Statewide Services; Loretta R. O'Brien, Librarian and Senior Assistant for Planning; and Tamiye Trejo, Northeast District Chief.

REFERENCES

Bayles, M. D. (1981). *Professional ethics.* Belmont, CA: Wadsworth.

City of Chicago, Department of Planning. (October 1988). *Chicago's changing population: Recent trends and Year 2000 projections.* Chicago: Author.

Fischer, R. G. (1986). Project ASIA: California public libraries serving the Asian community. *Library Journal, 111*(4), 62-64.

Hauptman, R. (1988). *Ethical challenges in librarianship.* Phoenix, AZ: Oryx Press.

Hoefer, M. D. (1989, June). *Recent immigrants: Their characteristics and places of residence.* Report of the Statistical Analysis Division, U. S. Immigration and Naturalization Service presented at the 108th Annual ALA Conference, Dallas, TX.

Lindsey, J. A. (1985). *Professional ethics and librarians.* Phoenix, AZ: Oryx Press.

Payne, J. (1988). Public libraries face California's ethnic and racial diversity. Rand Publication Series #3656. Santa Monica, CA: Rand Corporation.

Tarin, P. (1988). Rand misses the point: A "minority" report. *Library Journal, 113*(18), 31-34.

Trezza, A. F. (1986). Equal opportunity of access: A responsibility and a challenge. *Government Publications Review, 13*(1), 49-54.

KATHLEEN M. HEIM

Dean, Graduate School and
Professor, School of Library and Information Science
Louisiana State University
Baton Rouge, Louisiana

Human Resources Management: Ethics in Personnel

INTRODUCTION

**The Dilemma of the "Shared Fate" Vision versus a
Materialistic Society**

Ethics relating to human resources management in the library and information services profession must be viewed from a more comprehensive ethical stance at the outset. Since this conference is devoted to a wide range of ethical considerations, it seems appropriate to begin this discussion with some deliberation on career choice itself.

Those who embark on a career in library and information science are, for the most part, "service-oriented." Of students entering the field in 1988, 65.6 percent indicated that "service orientation" was "important" or "very important" to them. More materialistic concerns such as benefits (35.8 percent), salary (37.2 percent), and status (29.1 percent) were rated far less highly (Heim & Moen, 1989, p. 47). Given these motivations of entry-level librarians, it seems safe to characterize the field as one in which the ethos of "shared fate" has some credence. That is, all individual lives are so important that no individual can be exempted from joining in the task that secures conditions of self-realization for all people.

In his discussion of career selection, Norman S. Care (1987) has provided a provocative challenge to those seeking careers who live in affluent societies. His argument is complicated, but in essence he asserts,

> The notion that all human beings are equal members of a moral community and that their lives are bound up together is reflected in the recommendation that deliberations about careers are to be

101

seriously constrained by the value of service to others. Morality
requires, in these circumstances, a service career. (p. 40)

Librarianship is a career for which service has been an overriding
motivation for those who chose it. Insofar as arguments such as Care's
are developed, those in the field have made an ethical commitment—
perhaps the only just and right kind of commitment given the concept
of "shared fate"—to a life's work that is sustained by an inherent belief
that service is the socially responsible mode.

If this basic precept is considered as ethical personnel issues in
libraries are explored, it is clear that simple borrowing from corporate
personnel models may not be appropriate. After all, most of the
individuals who work in libraries do so with an articulate sense that
theirs is a service occupation. In light of this fundamental fact, it may
be difficult to superimpose personnel practices that govern for-profit
enterprises. Simply put, at the outset of any discussions of personnel
practices in libraries, it must be recognized that the library work force
is motivated by service.

How does a "service-motivated" work force differ from the work
force in general? Why should this be a consideration at all? In the
abstract, there are some generalizations that might be made. Salaries,
status, and benefits mean less than the opportunity to do meaningful
work. Thus these factors have historically been depressed for library
and information occupations.

Yet as society changes—unhappily for those who hold a "shared
fate" vision for humanity—the supply of librarians has diminished
(Moen & Heim, 1988). This might be for many reasons, but an especially
disturbing one to contemplate is that "service orientation" is shared by
a smaller pool. As the society at large has become more focused on
material gain, the low salaries and benefits long associated with librarianship have made it a less attractive career option. The dilemma is
that those who currently set salaries may be confounded since they
themselves are the product of a time when service-oriented work had
a broader appeal. While current entrants still espouse a proclivity to a
service-oriented field, the pool of like-minded individuals is shrinking.
If library administrators hope to recruit new personnel from a larger
pool, they will need to secure salaries and benefits that are more
competitive with other professions.

So at the outset of this presentation, the basic ethical dilemma of
personnel issues relating to librarianship as viewed by this author is one
of conflicting value orientations. Many who currently administer libraries
are searching for new entrants with a service orientation at a time when
the pool of individuals with this world-view is shrinking. Yet there has

never been a time when disparities in economic status have been greater among and within nations. It is a sad irony that at this time, when it is a moral imperative for those with career choices to choose service, fewer do so.

THE HUMAN RESOURCES MANAGEMENT FUNCTION: BROAD-BASED ORGANIZATIONAL CONCERNS

While the pool of workers with a service orientation is shrinking, provoking a framing ethical dilemma for library administrators, the problem of a diminishing work force in general has affected all employment sectors. In their overview of "Societal Trends and Staffing Policies," W. F. Cascio and R. F. Zammuto (1989) observe that the next three decades pose a major challenge to human resources managers due to an aging work force and a shrinking entry-level employee pool comprised of fewer highly educated and technically skilled workers at a time when organizations must be more innovative and responsive.

To combat these challenges, personnel work has become more sophisticated and a gradual terminological shift to the use of "human resources management" has taken place. The six areas of concern to the human resources management function within organizations are attraction (identifying job requirements and providing equal opportunity), selection, retention (sustaining motivation to perform work effectively and building a healthy work environment), development (preservation and enhancement of employees' competence), assessment (evaluation of job performance and compliance with organizational personnel policies), and adjustment (retirement and outplacement)(pp. 2-2 — 2-3).

Each of these areas of concern provides ethical dilemmas for human resources managers and will be discussed below. However, it is important to first identify areas of concern especially important to those in a library work place.

A recent survey of library administrators ranked "Need for confidentiality" and "Conflict between the rights of the individual and the rights of the institution" at the top of the list of most common ethical problems. These were followed by "Hiring practices and policies," "Fair treatment of employees," "Conflict between the rights of one individual and another," "Affirmative action/equal opportunity," "Discipline and discharge," and "Performance evaluation" (Ethics, 1988, p. 21).

Asked what were viewed as the most important ethical problems facing the profession as a whole, administrators cited "Confidentiality" and "Affirmative action" which tied for the top ranking (p. 22). These problems will be kept in mind as the organizational concerns relating to human resources management and ethics are discussed below. To give the discussion focus, the ethical issues already identified (Ethics, 1988) are examined.

Attraction/Recruitment

As has been pointed out in the introduction to this paper, "attraction" (or recruitment, as it is more often designated) is undergirded by the larger ethical dilemma facing society: the need for competent individuals to select service careers. The aspects of recruitment that library managers cited as posing the most compelling of all ethical problems are those relating to affirmative action and equal opportunity.

Although affirmative action has been eroded by recent Supreme Court decisions, it is heartening that library respondents view it as a top ethical issue relating to personnel. In her review of issues relating to minority recruitment in librarianship, Ann Knight Randall (1988) observed:

> The demographics of the U. S. population are changing. Within the next two decades, one in three U. S. residents will be a racial or ethnic minority. One of the key ways to serve these populations' information needs effectively is to increase the participation of minorities in library and information services. (p. 18)

However, the number of ethnic minorities entering the profession continues to be small as shown by the 1988 LISSADA Survey. Students entering the field in 1988 were 93.7 percent White, 3.7 percent Black, 1.1 percent Asian/Pacific, .8 percent Hispanic, and .6 percent American Indian (Heim & Moen, 1989, p. 89). These statistics have not improved greatly during the 1980s. If data from the LISSADA Survey of 1988 are compared to data from the COSWL Study of 1980, the fact that White representation has held steady, at 93.7 percent, demonstrates no improvement in the ethnic diversification of the profession during the 1980s (p. 149).

Human resources managers must grapple with affirmative action issues. However, adding a tag line to job announcements that the institution is an equal opportunity employer is not enough. It is time to re-examine this commitment and make it real. This is especially important in a milieu in which affirmative action has been criticized as reverse discrimination.

What are the arguments against affirmative action? Thomas Nagel (1983) has noted that it has been viewed as inefficient, unfair and damaging to self-esteem (pp. 483-85). "Inefficiency" objections may mean that there is some initial lowering of performance. "Unfairness" objections occur if a protected minority is selected over a more qualified member of the majority. However, affirmative action is a means of increasing the economic and social strength of formerly victimized groups. "Self-esteem" objections are difficult to overcome and certainly cause minorities who are fully competitive to fall under suspicion. However, given the small numbers of minorities in the profession, these objections still seem moot.

In thinking through commitment to affirmative action, one point deserves special emphasis: "The goal to be pursued is the reduction of a great social injustice, not proportional representation of the races in all institutions and professions" (p. 149). Those in human resources management need to review these ideas. By definition, the library profession fosters access to information. A diversification of the library work force contributes doubly to the correction of social injustice, both through application of strong affirmative action policies in hiring and through the creation of an environment that demonstrates the strengths of cultural diversity.

Selection

Issues relating to hiring policies and procedures were also ranked high among ethical concerns of library administrators. Confidentiality of references for job applicants and the requirement of the MLS for professional positions were specifically cited as problematic.

Confidentiality

Beth M. Paskoff (1987) has reviewed confidentiality as background for a study examining the use of letters of reference in hiring. She found great variety in attitudes toward confidentiality. Although her respondents claimed that waiving the right to access on the part of applicants was not necessary in letters of recommendation, more than half used telephone references for sensitive follow-ups.

Passage of the Family Education Rights and Privacy Act in 1974 established the right of job applicants to review letters of reference, although the Buckley Amendment established the right of colleges and universities to request that applicants waive their rights to send letters.

Issues of confidentiality do not end at the hiring stage, of course. They continue throughout the personnel process. Annual evaluations, personal problems (such as substance abuse), and terminations all have aspects of confidentiality that must be addressed.

By clearly establishing what aspects of personnel are confidential on behalf of the employee and which are confidential on behalf of the organization, future conflicts can be avoided. If an employee with a substance abuse problem, for example, uses organizational support to participate in an Employee Assistance Program, it would need to be made quite clear whether this information is so indicated on a personnel file. Without guarantees of confidentiality, most would probably decline such help, undercutting the viability of these programs.

In devising personnel policies relating to confidentiality, it is thus important to weigh and balance employee and organization rights. Increasingly, laws and court cases do make employee records available, necessitating that clear and carefully followed policies be developed for retention of files.

Requirement of the MLS

Partly due to shortages in the field and partly due to the fact that some positions may not appear to require the MLS, survey respondents indicated that the MLS requirement for professional positions sometimes caused ethical problems. Jane Robbins (1987) has reviewed the MLS requirement for professional positions. Her paper, developed for the American Library Association's Office for Library Personnel Resources, is a lucid and convincing argument for the MLS requirement. However, she does cite two concerns that must be confronted. One, the MLS requirement should not be stated as a minimum qualification unless the prospective employer has made a clear analysis of the position and determined that the position requires the knowledge, skills, and attitudes most effectively attainable through formal education. Second, when a position that has been systematically determined to be a professional position is challenged by a local, state or federal inquiry or legal action, the employing unit must steadfastly defend the minimum education requirement set (p. 18). Robbins' analysis is requisite reading for those concerned about the MLS requirement as an ethical issue, as she has made it clear that without thoughtful formulation of job descriptions and announcements, the MLS requirement may be challenged.

Retention

Retaining good employees is important to organizations. While some turnover cannot be helped, much can be attributed to avoidable factors such as wages, benefits, and working conditions. Negative aspects of turnover include disruption to operations, replacement costs, retraining, and lost productivity.

Aspects of retention with ethical implications include compensation and pay equity, conflict between individuals, conflict of personal integrity with the institution, and motivation. Retention is the product of an organization's capacity to sustain employee effectiveness and motivation.

Compensation and Pay Equity

Certainly, adequate compensation is a basic factor in employee retention. Low pay in the library profession has had some effect on the field's ability to attract sufficient numbers of new entrants and has caused others to leave for more lucrative positions.

Compensation management can positively affect organizations. Frederick Duda (1989) has observed that inadequate compensation leads to poor performance, absenteeism, excessive turnover and strikes (p. 106). He also identifies equity—both internal and external—as an important objective of compensation programs.

Pay equity raises many ethical issues. The fact that work in female-dominated occupations is compensated at lower rates than in male-dominated occupations has been abundantly documented. Actions to fight for pay equity in librarianship are delineated in the American Library Association's *Pay Equity Manual* (Kenady, 1989) and Topics in Personnel Kit #9: *Pay Equity: Issues and Strategies* (ALA, 1987). Pay equity is probably the central ethics issue relating to compensation. It is an issue that should concern employers in all sectors. Arguments that oppose pay equity can be stated quite succinctly: fair compensation of women would destroy the current economy. While much rhetoric abounds that attempts to blame the market for lower wages and salaries in female-dominated occupations, the truth is that fair compensation would require major adjustments in the economy. Thus movement toward pay equity has been slow.

However, if human resources managers in library settings elect to choose the ethical course, a top priority in each setting must be a personal and institutional commitment to pay equity issues. So long as public librarians earn less than other municipal workers with comparable education, so long as academic librarians earn less than faculty, so long as special librarians earn less than other corporate administrators, and so long as support staff in any library setting earn less than support staff in other settings, there are important ethical battles relating to compensation to be faced.

The struggle for pay equity must be viewed as a central ethical issue in librarianship. Failure to grapple with this problem would indicate a failure in personnel priorities.

Conflict between individuals

Stress and burnout, which contribute to turnover, are often attributable to poor interpersonal relations in the work place. Charles A. Bunge (1989) has noted that lack of recognition and respect coupled with such factors as "tension between professionals and nonprofessionals, competition for status and resources, irritable and negative coworkers and gossip" (pp. 95-96) are all stress producing. Many of these tensions can be traced to poor supervision, vagueness of job descriptions, lack of feedback, and conflicting job expectations.

Correction of these problems has ethical overtones in that it requires that administrators and human resources managers recognize the intrinsic quality of workers. Strong vertical organizations without mechanisms for feedback are most susceptible to this type of retention problem. Since correction of environments that foster poor interpersonal relations requires a management style that provides clear policies and seeks employee input, it will first require an administrative commitment to recognition of individual worth.

Motivation
  Closely tied to management styles that avoid conflict is the managerial attitude toward motivation. Charles A. Martell's (1989) excellent and concise summary of motivation theory distills this concept in a simple concluding statement: "The best advice is to treat your employees with respect and provide them with meaningful work; include an opportunity for them to discover and use an inner drive to make a contribution and to find recognition for their efforts" (p. 78).

  The ethical consideration here is the same that mandates better configured work environments for interpersonal relations: a basic recognition of the fact that each individual in an organization has drives that, when fostered, contribute to organizational effectiveness. This simple ethical decision—to recognize individual worth—destroys a "productivity" mentality, encourages commonly set goals, and creates an environment in which employees will wish to stay and contribute their best.

Conflict of personal integrity with the institution
  One additional problem that may impair retention is when an employee experiences a personal ethical conflict with the organization. While initially it might seem difficult to imagine examples in a library setting, there are certainly ethical problems at all levels.

  Consider the circulation clerk faced with a large fine to be levied on a patron who has been ill or hospitalized. A rigid bureaucracy might not allow the clerk to make the discretionary decision to waive the fine. Think of the children's department staff of a public library faced with "latch-key" children who must be turned away without parents in attendance in accordance with Board policy. Imagine the librarian in an academic library located at a religious university unable to provide information on abortion rights.

  There are countless examples of library situations wherein an employee's individual ethical stance may be in conflict with the organization's policies. The employee may choose to fight them, may resignedly accept them, or may simply seek employment elsewhere.

In any case, human resources managers must deploy their own ethical senses to provide clear and nonpunitive procedures for resolving ethical conflicts. Librarians in tenured positions may have built-in safeguards when faced with such dilemmas, but those without the protection of academic freedom may be placed in untenable situations.

There is a growing concern for ethical behavior in the business world. A recent study of employers of MBA students in Detroit tested the "Ethics/Integrity" dimension of managers. This dimension was defined as "Demonstrating a system of moral principles or values commensurate with America's Judeo-Christian background and laws, and showing that those principles or values are used in evaluating management decisions and actions" (Mortensen et al., 1989, p. 255).

Results found employers rating ethics and integrity as "moderate to somewhat important." Examples of ethical behavior provided to respondents included "personal ethics" (not compromising one's own standards; providing accurate information to employees, critics, and the public; considering the rights of others in decision-making); "codified ethics" (organization standards of behavior; adhering to laws and regulations; knowing what constitutes acceptable and unacceptable work practices); "ethical analysis" (analyzing the ethical or moral ramifications of problems or issues; evaluating decisions based on their long-term effects on society); and "activist ethics" (refusing to accept dishonest or questionable actions; willing to "blow the whistle" on unethical practices). Among these four types of ethical behavior, codified ethics ranked highest, followed by personal ethics, activist ethics, and ethical analysis.

Given the broader concern about ethics in society, and especially the results of a cross-industry study of businesses as summarized above, it seems safe to predict that instances where individual ethics conflict with the organization are more likely to be discussed, analyzed, and assessed in an open environment. Such action will contribute to fewer retention problems relating to ethical conflicts between the individual and the employing organization. However, it is critical that receptivity to such discussion be conveyed by managers.

Development

What ethical problems surround the staff development function? Certainly several surround selection. Who should be provided development opportunities? Libraries routinely provide scattershot support of professional staff to attend conferences as interest arises. Should the employee choose or should the organization? Should support staff receive similar opportunities? Should staff be allowed to participate in development opportunities that may provide them with skills and knowledge to move on and apply for other positions in other organizations? Should development opportunities be rewards for those who have been good organizational players?

Embedded in the questions above are some ethical concerns. A human resources manager must develop policies for staff development or individuals will be supported for development for indiscriminate reasons. Without policies that undergird development activities, funds could easily be used without a strong objective basis.

The organization's administration needs to decide if it will take a chance and provide opportunities that move the individual up and out. Clearly, without a well-delineated policy on goals for staff development, there is much room for ad hoc decision-making vis-a-vis the development function.

A commitment to staff development means that extant personnel resources can be used. Without staff development programs—given the rate of change in today's libraries—current staff will not be able to accommodate new technologies and procedures (Lipow, 1989, p. 88). The ethical aspect of development programs is inherent, once again, in a firm belief that staff are individuals with inner motivations and drives that need to be fostered, not interchangeable parts.

Assessment

Performance evaluation or assessment was cited as posing ethical problems in the LPN survey, but the actual conduct of such reviews, if well conceived, should not place evaluators in difficult positions. Lucy R. Cohen (1989) has recently summarized possible difficulties that surround performance evaluations: the "halo" effect (overall positive evaluation based on excellence in one aspect of a job); the "pitchfork" effect (overall negative evaluation based on poor performance in one aspect of a job); "central" tendency (rating everyone average); "loose" (rating everyone high); "tight" (rating everyone low); "recency" (rating on latest performance); "length of service" (rating those with longevity high); and "competitive" (rating as a result of how the rater has been evaluated) (pp. 41-42). However, these problems are not so much ethical as the result of unclear procedural evaluation or lack of policies.

As with so many other personnel issues that at the outset seem to present "ethical" problems, the real problem is one of omission. This omission is of clear and well-publicized policies and procedures as well as failure to recognize the intrinsic worth of individuals. These are the crux of most ethics issues vis-a-vis personnel.

Adjustment

Outplacement, terminations, and retirement place necessary requirements on human resources managers. In cases of resignations or retirements, a good personnel manual will provide guidelines for a smooth and orderly passing of responsibilities.

Terminations and outplacements, of course, are another matter. "Outplacement" is the term generally used when an organization is "downsizing" and a requisite "reduction in force" must take place.

Termination, on the other hand, does require ethical considerations. In a good discussion of "employment at will" — standard practice in the private sector — Jeanne Isacco (1988) observed that, while there should be mechanisms to discharge employees who are not adequate to their jobs, "it is not in the public good, nor is it humane, just and tolerant for a public employer to abandon these values for the sake of comfort and convenience, even though it may be legal" (pp. 19-20).

Wrongful discharge suits may be avoided by five steps:

1) Review employee manuals and handbooks to delete statements that imply a contractual relationship. Avoid, in particular, reference to "permanent employment," employment based on "satisfactory performance," or statements that dismissal will be only for "cause."
2) Inform supervisors and interviewers not to make oral promises about the duration of employment.
3) Evaluate performance according to objective standards.
4) Adopt fair and evenly applied work rules and disciplinary procedures.
5) Institute a formal grievance process (Employment, 1988, pp. 20-21).

As in all other aspects of human resources management, great care must be given to apply procedures fairly and objectively. There is good evidence that employees with any grievance history may be negatively perceived even when their cause is just. In a study of public sector organization's grievances between 1979 and 1985, Brian S. Klaas (1989) found that individual work histories did have an impact on subsequent grievance procedures. Certainly, employee recognition of negative treatment when due process is accorded impacts the use mode of these processes. It is simply not ethical to establish these processes and penalize those who avail themselves of those same processes.

A survey of grievance procedures conducted by the ALA Office for Library Personnel Resources in 1988 found respondents positive about the fairness of procedures but negative about adversarial relationships created by their use. Great care must be used to apply these in a spirit of objectivity (Resolving Employee . . . , 1988).

Professional codes and personnel ethics

The cornerstone of ethical concerns for any is a code of ethics. As this conference demonstrates, ours is an era of renewed interest by the profession and the public-at-large on ethical considerations. In a review of the impact of professional codes of ethics, Mark S. Frankel (1989) has noted:

> In recent years, a blend of economic, social, legal and political events has had a profound effect not only on the behavior and performance of professionals, but also on the public's expectation of them. The days of unquestioned admiration on the part of clients or the general public are past. . . . It is quite timely for a reassessment of the professionals' moral role in society and, specifically, of codes of ethics from the perspectives of why, how, and with what impact. (p. 109)

In keeping with a societal concern about ethics, the American Library Association's Committee on Professional Ethics is now developing interpretive statements for each of the points in the ALA Code of Ethics (Ethics, p. 22).

CONCLUSION

This paper has sought to explore *particular* ethical issues identified as important by library administrators within the context of current thinking about human resources management. There are, of course, many more. It seems sensible that ongoing analysis of ethical personnel issues be monitored by the professional associations.

New issues arise every day. In their review of ethical issues raised by information technology, Lawson Crowe and Susan H. Anthes (1988) comment upon the need for personnel with a commitment to information provision. John Olsgaard (1989) has also observed that employee supervision may be impacted by the use of automated systems to track productivity.

Technology will need to be tempered by moral commitment to individual rights and worth. Legal and technical environments may change but at the heart of the matter, untouched by shifting background, must lie a reasoned and humane commitment to a just society.

REFERENCES

Bunge, C. A. (1989). Stress in the library workplace. *Library Trends, 38*(Summer), 92-102.

Care, N. S. (1987). *On sharing fate.* Philadelphia: Temple University Press.

Cascio, W. F., & Zammuto, R. F. (1989). Societal trends and staffing policies. In W. F. Cascio (Ed.), *Human resource planning, employment and placement* (pp. 2-30). Washington, DC: Bureau of National Affairs.

Cohen, L. R. (1989). Conducting performance evaluations. *Library Trends, 38*(Summer), 40-52.

Crowe, L., & Anthes, S. H. (1988). The academic librarian and information technology: Ethical issues. *College and Research Libraries, 49*(2), 123-130.

Duda, F. (1989). Developing compensation systems in academic libraries. *Library Trends, 38*(1), 103-126.

Employment at will. (1988). *Library Personnel News, 2*(2), 20-21.

Ethics and personnel. (1988). *Library Personnel News, 2*(2), 21-22.

Frankel, M. S. (1989). Professional codes: Why, how and with what impact? *Journal of Business Ethics, 8*(February/March), 109-115.

Godzins Lipow, A. (1989). Training for change: Staff development in a new age. *Journal of Library Administration, 10*(1), 87-89.

Heim, K. M., & Moen, W. E. (1989). *Occupational entry.* Chicago: ALA.

Isacco, J. (1988). Public sector ethics differ. *Library Personnel News, 2*(2), 19-20.

Kenady, C. (1989). *Pay equity: An action manual for library workers.* Chicago: ALA.

Klaas, B. S. (1989). Managerial decision making about employee grievances: The impact of the grievant's work history. *Personnel Psychology, 42*(Spring), 53-68.

Martell, C. A. (1989). Achieving high performance in library work. *Library Trends, 38*(1), 73-91.

Moen, W. E., & Heim, K. M. (Eds.). (1988). *Librarians for the new millennium.* Chicago: ALA.

Mortensen, R. A.; Smith, J. E.; & Cavanagh, G. F. (1989). The importance of ethics to job performance: An empirical investigation of managers' perceptions. *Journal of Business Ethics, 8*(April), 255.

Nagel, T. (1983). A defense of affirmative action. In T. L. Beauchamp & N. E. Bowie (Eds.), *Ethical theory and business* (pp. 483-85). Englewood Cliffs, NJ: Prentice-Hall.

Olsgaard, J. N. (1989). The physiological and managerial impact of automation on libraries. *Library Trends, 37*(4), 484-494.

Paskoff, B. M. (1987, February). *Letters of reference in the hiring practices of ARL libraries.* Paper presented at the Library Science Colloquium, Florida State University, Tallahassee, FL.

Pay equity: Issues and strategies. (1987). Chicago: ALA.

Randall, A. K. (1988). Minority recruitment in librarianship. In W. E. Moen & K. M. Heim (Eds.), *Librarians for the new millennium* (p. 18). Chicago: ALA.

Resolving employee grievances. (1988). *Library Personnel News, 2*(4), 49-51.

Robbins, J. (1987, December). *Master's degree from a programme accredited by the American Library Association required.* A background paper on the value of the master's degree in librarianship commissioned by the ALA Office of Library Personnel Resources Advisory Committee. Chicago: ALA.

ROBERT WENGERT

Professor of Philosophy
University of Illinois at Urbana-Champaign

Some Ethical Questions for Consideration and Discussion

[*Editor's note:* The final session of this conference, perhaps the highlight of the entire event, was not a formal paper. Professor Wengert facilitated a discussion among participants of some ethical questions he had formulated. The questions had been presented to them at the time of registration, so they had been given the opportunity to consider their stance before the discussion occurred. The questions are reproduced here in the hope that they will be of use to others leading discussions on ethical issues.

Before Professor Wengert led the discussion, he introduced some general principles relating to ethics, as follows.]

What Ethics Is Not

1. Whatever religious authorities say
2. Whatever legal authorities say
3. Whatever public opinion is

Some Substitutes for "Hard Thinking" in Ethics

1. Absolutism. Things that are right or wrong are always right or wrong. Circumstances make no difference.
2. Relativism. What is right or wrong depends entirely on how one feels about some matter. What is right for one person could be wrong for another in exactly the same situation.

Some Styles of Reasoning in Ethics

1. Result theories (consequentialist, teleological): An action is determined to be right or wrong by whether its results or consequences

are good or bad. An example is *utilitarianism:* One should do what will bring about the greatest welfare of all concerned.

2. Nonconsequentialist theories (deontological): Certain things ought (or ought not) to be done regardless of their consequences. An example is *contractualism:* An act is wrong if it violates those constraints which any rational person, considering the matter in a way which favors no one's particular interests, would agree should be imposed.

ETHICAL QUESTIONS

These appear as a series of statements or of actual questions with which one can agree or fail to agree. They formed the basis for a spirited discussion at the conference and revealed wide differences of opinion among the participants.

1. Is it all right to say, "$100,000 represents my top offer for this property," when indeed it does not?
2. Is it all right to say, "$100,000 is what you owe us for our services," when indeed it is not?
3. If the government has fixed the highway speed at 55 miles per hour, is it wrong (immoral, unethical) to drive at 60 mph on the highway?
4. If the government has fixed the emission rate for a chemical from your library's heating system at 55 parts per billion, would it be wrong for you to increase the emission rate to 60 ppb?
5. A student asks for help on a topic for Professor Wengert's class. You find something on a reference database. He thanks you. You overhear him saying to a friend that he is downloading this information, printing it out, and handing it in to Prof. Wengert as his own. Should you say something to Prof. Wengert, whom you know, about this?
6. A week after the event described in question number 5, Prof. Wengert comes to you and says that he suspects one of the students in his class of plagiarizing. He asks if you would know where the student may have gotten the information. Should you tell Prof. Wengert the truth?
7. Three of your staff at the reference desk have begun to wear pro-choice buttons while serving patrons. You tell them not to wear the buttons while working at the reference desk. They say you have treated them unethically by depriving them of their right of free speech. Have you?
8. A lawyer representing the plaintiff in a complicated suit has worked with you in the law library for about a week tracking down obscure

but relevant material. In gratitude for your help, the lawyer has shared with you some references and modes of cross-reference with which you had been unfamiliar. The next week, the lawyer for the defendant asks if you could help him find information on the case. You do not mention its source, but you immediately give him all the information you got from the plaintiff's lawyer. Is this unethical?

9. Credit companies regularly call the library requesting information from the city directory about names of the neighbors of a person whose account is delinquent. Library policy is to refuse to give out such information. Is this unethical?

10. The situation is the same as for question number 9, but this time the agent for the company comes to the library and asks to use the city directory. The agent is always shown where the directory is and even how to use it if help is needed. Is this unethical?

11. Neighbors of the library have requested that it join them in protesting the plan to open a massage parlor in a building just two doors down from the library. You refuse to join the protest on the grounds that a library must remain neutral on controversial issues. Are you right?

12. An arson has occurred locally. At the site, firefighters have discovered a bookbag they think might have been used by the arsonist. The bag is burnt but two of the books are identifiably from your library. You are asked to supply the name of the patron who has the books charged out. You refuse to do so on grounds that it will violate the patron's privacy. Is that the right decision?

13. A young girl has recently been murdered. On her body was found a picture about satanic cults. The picture had come from a fairly recent issue of a news magazine. In the return cart of your library, you see that issue of the magazine. It appears that some pages may have been cut out of it. You decide that investigating it more carefully might compromise the privacy of a patron. You ignore it. Did you do the right thing?

14. Several patrons have requested that the library purchase a diet book which experts in reviews have identified as dangerous to the health of anyone who follows the diet. You decide not to order the book. Is this unethical?

15. Your library charges fees for the use of records, videos, films, databases and recent best-selling books, but there is no fee for other books or magazines. Are you being unfair in your treatment of patrons who prefer audio-visual materials and bestsellers?

16. You are asked by the local police chief and the FBI to tell them of any individuals or groups who request materials on supercomputers and also to tell them of any individuals or groups who ask about

others using the materials on supercomputers. You readily agree. Are you being unethical?

17. You are asked by the local ACLU chapter and the ALA to tell them of any individuals or groups who are requesting information about others using material in the library. Is this unethical?

18. As an academic librarian, when the President of the University makes a request, you clearly handle it more quickly and carefully than you would have had the request been made by an undergraduate. Is this wrong?

19. As a medical librarian, you will give a caller the definition of a technical medical term having to do with their health, but when they further ask what that means and why their doctor might be testing them for that, you refer them to their physician even when you know the answer perfectly well. Is this the right thing to do?

20. As a reference librarian, you will give a caller the definition of a technical legal term having to do with their welfare rights, but when they further ask what that means and what they are supposed to do about it, you refer them to their attorney even when you know the answer perfectly well. Is this right of you to do?

21. You charge more than cost on the copy machine so that you can get enough money to purchase some serials you otherwise could not afford. Is this ethical of you?

22. An employee of your public library has been convicted of child abuse. This took place in another town and did not involve a library patron. He has been placed on probation. His action and conviction have been widely publicized and many people are upset that the judge let him off so lightly. He does his job for your library well. Should you fire him?

23. Answer the following questions as simply and directly as you can:
    a) When you say an action is wrong, what do you mean?
    b) When you say an action is "the right thing to do," what do you mean?

24. Mention one or two of the highest terms of praise you can imagine for another human whom you know.

25. Mention one or two of the strongest terms of criticism you can imagine using of another person whom you know.

CONTRIBUTORS

CHARLES A. BUNGE is a faculty member at the School of Library and Information Studies of the University of Wisconsin-Madison, where he teaches in the areas of reference and information services, library cooperation and networking, and collection development. He is the author of numerous articles in the professional literature, especially in the area of evaluation of reference services. He is active in professional associations, including having served as President of the Reference and Adult Services Division of the American Library Association. He has provided consulting and continuing education services for reference staffs and library organizations throughout the country.

CLIFFORD G. CHRISTIANS is Research Professor of Communications at the University of Illinois at Urbana-Champaign, Director of the Institute of Communications Research and head of the doctoral program in communications. He received his Ph.D. in communications from the University of Illinois, and has been a visiting scholar in philosophical ethics at Princeton and in social ethics at the University of Chicago. He is co-author of *Jacques Ellul: Interpretive Essays* (University of Illinois Press, 1981) and of *Media Ethics: Cases and Moral Reasoning* (3rd ed.) (Longman, 1991).

DONNA M. GOEHNER is Dean of University Libraries at Western Illinois University. She holds a master's degree and a certificate of advanced study in library science from the University of Illinois and a Ph.D. in education from Southern Illinois University. Her publications include articles on acquisitions and budgeting in *The Serials Librarian, Technical Services Quarterly,* and *Collection Management.* She also contributed a chapter on ethics of working with vendors which recently appeared in the book *Understanding the Business of Library Acquisitions* (ALA, 1990).

ROBERT HAUPTMAN holds a doctorate in comparative literature and is an Associate Professor at St. Cloud State University, where he does reference work and teaches library science. The author of some 300 books, essays, articles, and reviews, he recently edited a forthcoming issue of *Library Trends* and is currently coauthoring *Technology and Information Services* for Ablex Publishing.

KATHLEEN M. HEIM is Dean of the Graduate School at Louisiana State University and was previously Dean of the School of Library and

Information Science at the same institution. From 1978-1983 she served on the faculty at the University of Illinois at Urbana-Champaign. She has edited *RQ, Public Libraries,* and two issues of *Library Trends.* Her most recent book is *Adult Services: An Enduring Focus* (1990) published by ALA.

F. W. LANCASTER, co-director of this Allerton Institute, is a Professor of Library and Information Science at the University of Illinois and the editor of *Library Trends.* He is the author of eight books in the field of library/information science.

SAMUEL F. MORRISON is the Director of the Broward County Library system in Fort Lauderdale, Florida. He served as Chief Librarian for the City of Chicago during the planning and initial construction phase of the city's new central library. He is active in the American Library Association (ALA) and is a former president of the Florida Library Association. His MLS is from the University of Illinois at Urbana-Champaign.

GERALD R. SHIELDS is Associate Professor Emeritus, School of Information and Library Science, State University of New York-Buffalo. He received a master of arts in library science from the University of Wisconsin and is currently editor of feature articles in *Public Libraries,* the journal of the Public Library Association. He has served twelve years on the ALA Council and most recently was chair of the Professional Ethics Committee at ALA. He has published widely and was the recipient of the 1984 New York Library Association's Intellectual Freedom Award. He was the founding editor of *American Libraries* and the award-winning *Ohio Library Association Bulletin.*

ROBERT G. WENGERT is Associate Professor in the Department of Philosophy at the University of Illinois at Urbana-Champaign. He studied at the Pontifical Institute of Mediaeval Studies in Toronto and received his Ph.D. in philosophy from the University of Toronto. He teaches and writes on the history of philosophy (ancient and medieval), on informal and formal logic, and on ethics. He has written two computer programs for introductory logic courses, *Philo the Logician* and *Barbara the Syllogizer* (Madison: University of Wisconsin); *Philo* has recently won an international prize for software in philosophy. For the past eleven years he has taught sessions on Business Ethics for the Executive Development Center of the College of Commerce at UIUC. He has been invited to give presentations on professional ethics to numerous groups including CPAs, librarians, scientists, and managers at such places as Argonne National Laboratory and Research Triangle Park, North Carolina.

MICHAEL B. WESSELLS is community library coordinator for a five-county rural library district in western Washington. He holds an MLS from the University of North Carolina at Chapel Hill. Following public library stints in Ohio, he served for five years as a public library consultant at Battelle Memorial Institute, where he co-authored several research reports and the book *Working with Library Consultants* (Library Professional Publications, 1984).

HERBERT S. WHITE has been Professor at the Indiana University School of Library and Information Science since 1975 and served as Dean of the school from 1980 until 1990. Prior to his academic appointment, he was active in the administration of libraries and information organizations in the corporate and government sectors. The author of five books and more than 150 articles, Professor White writes and speaks frequently on issues of library administration and personnel management, and writes a column for *Library Journal*.

INDEX

Ahlerich, Milt, 20, 84-85
ALA Office for Intellectual Freedom, 23
ALA Office for Library Personnel Resources, 106, 111-12
ALA-reported library visits by FBI, 24
Allerton Institute, 1, 83
Almagno, Stephen, 83
American Association of Law Librarians, 83
Andersonville Trial, The, 35
Anthes, Susan H., 112
Art History Institute (Florence, Italy), 87
Atom bomb, ethical considerations about, 33

Bailey, Byron J., 88
Bar-Hillel, Yehoshua, 35, 37
Bayles, Michael D., 45-47, 54, 56, 58
Blake, Fay, 38
Blanke, Henry, 39
Blume, Judy, 36
Bonhoeffer, Dietrich, 14
Book selection and *de facto* censorship. *See* Censorship
Broderick, Dorothy, 46, 52-53
Buchanan, R. A., 7
Buckley Amendment, 105
Bunge, Charles A., 107
Burger, Robert, 2

Cantekin, Erdim I., 89
Cascio, W. F., 103
Censorship: and ethics, 36-37; book selection and *de facto* censorship, 86
Chu, Paul C. W., 88-89
Citizens Against Rampant Pornography (CARP), 66
Code of ethics for librarians: ALA, 112; history of, 22-23
Cohen, Lucy R., 110
Colaianni, Lois Ann, 89
Columbia University and the FBI Library Awareness Program, 19. *See also* FBI Library Awareness Program

Confidentiality and ethics, 84-85. *See also* Human Resources Management
Conflict resolution: 63-71; case studies of, 64-70; and censorship, 69-70; and fundamentalist concepts, 67-68; steps in, 64
Cook, M. Kathleen, 51
COSWL survey (1980), 104
Crowe, Lawson, 112

Dow Chemical Corporation, 33-34
Duda, Frederick, 107

Edwards, Don, 85
Ellul, Jacques, 4-5, 8
Employee turnover. *See* Human Resources Management: retention
Employee Assistance Program, 106
Employer-employee conflicts, 33-34
Ethical Challenges in Librarianship, 83
Ethical responsibility v. patriotic duty, 23-27
Ethics: definition of, 93; general principles of, 115; general questions about, 116-18; history of, 31-32; and organizational/client/professional loyalty, 39-41
Ethics and censorship. *See* Censorship
Everett, John H., 90
Exxon Corporation, 34

Family Education Rights and Privacy Act, 105
Farley, Judith, 52
FBI Library Awareness Program: 1, 19-30, 84-85; and Columbia University, 19; and multinational databases, 26-27; and Queens College, 21, 25
Fee-based services, ethical considerations for reference librarians, 53-54
Fees charged to corporate libraries, ethical considerations regarding, 39
Flowers, Helen F., 20
Fox, James, 20